The Eternal

Told and Untold stories of Shivaji Maharaj

By : Mihir Sane

Mihir Sane

<u>**The Eternal King**</u>

<u>**Told and Untold stories of Shivaji Maharaj***</u>

1st Paperback Edition
Impish Lass Publishing House
Published: 2020

Copyright: The Impish Lass Publishing House

Cover page photograph by- Avadhoot Bhat

Graphic design by - Meghal Walendra

Printed at – The Impish Lass Publishing House, Mumbai.

About the Author

Mihir Sane is the author of *"The Eternal King - Told and Untold stories of Shivaji Maharaj"* It is his first book. He is 8 years old and lives in New Jersey, USA. He loves playing chess and cricket. He loves theatre. But he loves reading the book most. Although he lives in the USA, he is deeply fascinated by Indian history. One day, he received a gift from his aunt. It was an Amar Chitra Katha book on Shivaji Maharaj. He was impressed by the bravery of this great king. He did not stop at this one book. He was so fascinated by Shivaji Maharaj that he started reading more books about him. He read 'Shivaji, the great maratha' by the famous author Ranjit Desai. He also read other books written in Marathi and English by various authors. Finally, the moment came, when he was ready to read the most famous book ever written about Shivaji Maharaj. That is 'Raja Shivachatrapati', by Babasaheb Purandare. He along with his dad read this book. Although he was far away from the place where all these great stories took place, these books brought him closer to those events and brave men. He could not stop talking about Shivaji Maharaj for months. He noticed not many friends around him here in the USA know about Shivaji Maharaj. Mihir decided to write the stories of Shivaji Maharaj for all those kids. He spent his summer break writing the book and drawing pictures for all the stories. He put his soul into writing this book at such a young age. He is still learning about Indian history. He is enjoying reading and learning everyday. He hopes that you enjoy reading this book.

First readers

Madhura Sane
Rushikesh Sane
Ashutosh Hadap and his family
Atul Chavan and his family
Taniya Kuber and her mom and dad

Special thanks to Aai and Baba !

The Maratha empire at the time of Shivaji Maharaj

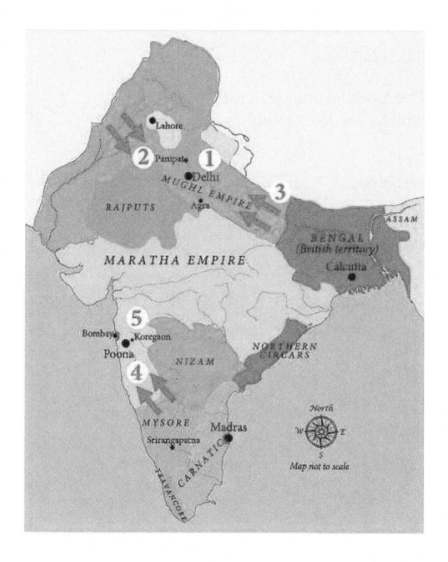

Table of Contents

About the Author I

First readers III

The Maratha empire at the
time of Shivaji Maharaj IV

Chapter 1
Bal Shivaji 1

Chapter 2
Dadoji Kondadev 3

Chapter 3
Forming the army. 5

Chapter 4
Torna 7

Chapter 5
Murarbaji joins the army. 9

Chapter 6
Veer Baji Jedhe 11

Chapter 7
Shivaji defeats Fateh Khan. 14

Chapter 8
Afzal Khan gets tricked. 16

Chapter 9

Baji Prabhu Deshpande. 19

Chapter 10

Battle of Umberkhind. 22

Chapter 11

**Shahistya Khan won
Sangram Durg.** 24

Chapter 12

Shahistya Khan 27

Chapter 13

Looting of Surat. 29

Chapter 14

Shahaji Raje dies. 31

Chapter 15

Murarbaji 33

Chapter 16

Mirza Raje Jaisingh and Shivaji meet. 36

Chapter 17

Escape from Agra. 39

Chapter 18

Attack on Portugese army. 41

Chapter 19

Janjira Fort 43

Chapter 20

Sambhaji and Shah Alam. 45

Chapter 21

Tanaji Malusare 47

Chapter 22

Battle of Salher. 50

Chapter 23

Second attack on Surat. 52

Chapter 24

Battle of Dindori. 54

Chapter 25

Shivaji wins Panhala from Siddi Jauhar. 56

Chapter 26

Bahlol Khan is captured. 58

Chapter 27

Prataprao Gujar 60

Chapter 28

Bahlol Khan runs away. 63

Chapter 29

Diler Khan runs away. 65

Chapter 30

Shivaji wins Pandavgad. 67

Chapter 31

Shivaji is crowned. 69

Chapter 32

Demise of Jijamata. 73

Chapter 33

Mohammad Quli Khan returns to Shivaji. 75

Chapter 34

First loot of Bahadur Khan Kokaltash. 78

Chapter 35

Padmadurg 80

Chapter 36

Second looting of Bahadur Khan. 82

Chapter 37

Janjira one more time. 84

Chapter 38

Nagoji Jedhe 86

Chapter 39

**Meeting Qutub Shah and Yesaji's
fight with the elephant.** 89

Chapter 40

Jinji 92

Chapter 41

Vyankoji Raje defeats Santaji. 94

Chapter 42
Capturing of Vyankoji Raje...97

Chapter 43
Sambhaji joins Diler Khan....99

Chapter 44
Death of Shivaji Maharaj...101

Chapter 1

Bal Shivaji

The sun was setting when drums started to play in Shivneri fort. The news spread fast that a baby boy was born to Jijabai. Her husband Shahaji Raje was fighting for Shah Jahan. In the fort the main god of the fort was Lord Shivai so Jijabai and her maids decided to name the baby after Shivai. They decided to name him Shiva which is another name of Shankar, the Indian god. Shiva later was called Shivaji by everyone around him.

Shivaji was growing day by day. He was loved by everyone in the fort. Shivaji now grew and became 4. Every day Jijamata would tell him stories from the great Mahabharata or Ramayana. Shivaji would ask a lot of questions. When he turned 5, he and his friends would play with wooden weapons. He had a lot of friends. Yesaji Kank, Tanaji Malusare, Suryaji Malusare, Suryaji Kakte, Baji Pasalkar, Kudtoji Gujar, Netoji Palkar, Hansaji Mohitte were some of his best friends. Shivaji would make teams amongst his friends. He would be the leader of one group and battle with the other group. Shivaji's team always used to emerge victorious.

One day Jijamata was watching Shivaji and his friends. They were playing with their swords and shields. While playing this game, some of his friends surrounded him and asked him to surrender. But Shivaji was not afraid and did not want to surrender. He quickly took swords in both hands and started swinging them skillfully. His friends had to move back. Everyone was fighting as if it was a real battle. One of his friends was going to strike Shivaji's sword when Shivaji blocked him quickly. But Shivaji's sword went in the air and fell. Shivaji was very quick on his feet. He picked up his friend's sword lying on the ground and started hitting the other friend's shield. Shivaji and his friends were totally engrossed in playing this pretend battle for a long time. Jijabai who was watching all this was impressed with Shivaji's skills and dedication. She decided to get a teacher who could guide Shivaji.

Chapter 2

Dadoji Kondadev

Jijamata had found the right teacher for Shivaji. That time Shahaji Raje had also just come and helped Jijamata decide the right teacher for Shivaji. The teacher's name was Dadoji Kondadev. When Shivaji had moved to Lal Mahal, he met Dadoji Kondadev for the first time. He met him in 1637. Dadoji taught Shivaji how to read, write, use a sword, ride on a horse, and shoot. He used to do practice battles with Shivaji. He not only taught him battle tactics but he also helped Shivaji become a better person. He taught him how to be fair and never lie. Dadoji also taught Shivaji how to win battles with only a few soldiers using Guerrilla warfare.

He was Dadoji's best student.

At that time, Shahaji Raje was trying to give freedom to Maharashtra but the Nizam attacked Pune and destroyed Pune. When Shivaji reached Pune, he saw it was in a wreck. Dadoji took a lot of care of Pune. He fixed the broken houses, planted trees, and made sure everyone was taken care of. He made sure that everyone was treated fairly. Shahaji Raje asked Dadoji to take care of Pune and protect it from the outsiders.

Dadoji Kondadev loved watching Shivaji do small battles with Vishwasrao and others. Dadoji helped Shivaji build his army. Dadoji Kondadev died in 1649 but his work was honored. Shivaji Maharaj always paid his respect to Dadoji and gave all the credit of his skills to him.

Chapter 3

Forming the army.

S hivaji did not like Adil Shah and Shah Jahan. He knew they came
from Afghanistan and he did not like people who attacked his
country, Hindustan, like Mummuni, the king of Arabia who attacked
an Indian king named Lalitaditya or the Kushanas who were from
China, the enemies of the Gupta empire. Shivaji hated how Adil Shah
and Shah Jahan would just come to Maharashtra and loot people,
kill people, capture the sardars, and burn houses. He did not like
the way they treated common people. He did not like how common
people were suffering because of these kings. Shivaji was very kind
and wanted to help these people, free them from these kings. He
wanted everyone to feel safe in their own country.

One day, he gathered his friends together. Shivaji told his friends not to tell anyone. He told his friends, "We will not remain slaves of the mean and wicked Adil Shah and Shah Jahan. We need to get them out of our country. So who's with me?" All the friends agreed. Shivaji's speech was so inspiring that his little army started growing day by day. He was a true friend so all his friends joined him in this noble mission. Vishwasrao also also agreed to help them with his army. Even Dadoji Kondadev gave Shivaji his blessings and helped their army to learn battle techniques.

Shivaji decided to take an oath in Raireshwar temple. Shivaji met a blacksmith named Bhima. Bhima decided to make swords for them. After Bhima gave them the swords, Shivaji went to Rairashwer. At Raireshwar he took a sword and held it up. He made a small wound on his finger and then all his friends got up and sought blessings of Lord Raireshwar. Shivaji took the oath on 27th of April 1645. This is the day when Shivaji and his friends decided to free their beloved country and establish Swarajya (their own kingdom), the kingdom of the people. This was just the beginning; the beginning of something amazing, extraordinary.

Chapter 4

Torna

It had been almost two years since the oath. Shivaji and his trusted friends were practicing and polishing their skills tirelessly under the guidance of Dadoji Kondadev. Shivaji had moved to Pune and started living in Lal Mahal. He used to look at Torna from Lal Mahal. He sent Bahirji Naik to see how much army there was in Torna. Shivaji told Jijamata, "Stay near the foothills of Torna. We will blow a cannon and when you hear it, come with your horse to Torna."

Bahirji Naik went in disguise and started walking around the whole fort. There were 200 soldiers. One of the guards had a doubt about him. He ordered the army to catch him. Bahirji Naik ran away but 150 people ran after him. Shivaji took his 500 soldiers and went on to Torna. The guards shot arrows at them but it did not stop them. Shivaji left 300 guards to fight them. He took 200 soldiers and put ladders to Torna. They climbed up Torna. The soldiers of Torna fought them but the 200 people surrounded the 50 people and made them surrender. The fort keeper was taking a nap and was woken by the sound. He went out to fight but Shivaji made him surrender. It was the first ever fort won by Shivaji and his army. It was a first step towards a huge kingdom. Jijabai was delighted to see Shivaji's vision, and bravery, Then Shivaji raised the saffron flag.

After winning Torna, Shivaji realized that the castle was ruined and he fixed it. While fixing it he found a pot full of money. They used that money to build a fort called Rajgadh.

Chapter 5

Murarbaji joins the army.

Shivaji won Torna and now he wanted to win Jawli. The Mores were most known for the Chandrarao branch in history. His capital was at Jawali. The area of then Jawali Jagir was from Raigad Fort to Fort Vishalgad. Daulatrao More was the successor of Chandrarao title. He was ruling the Jawali area. He had now become old. He did not have any sons. His wife Manakabai adopted Yashwantrao More from the original family stock to keep the title. Yashwantrao More became the fort keeper after the death of Daulatrao More. Yashwantrao More now inherited the title of Chandrarao and started ruling Jawali area.

Shivaji asked him to hand over the fort to Swarajya. But Chandrarao did not want to because he thought that he was now the king of Jawli.

He was serving as a Mansabdar of Adil Shah. One day Shivaji wrote a letter saying, "Please give me Jawli, I will give you a lot of money and respect." The subedar of Jawli did not listen. He wrote a letter to Shivaji saying, "Who are you to decide? I have such an army that I can attack you and wipe out your whole power." Shivaji got mad and took 1,000 of his soldiers. Chandrarao More's army ran away. Shivaji saw a brave opponent soldier. He was fighting vigorously. Shivaji ordered his 100 soldiers to go fight with that brave soldier and kept 900 soldiers to keep fighting alongside him. Shivaji saw the brave soldier directing his huge army towards him. He decided to use the guerilla war technique. He hid in the dense Jawali jungle with his army and attacked the opponents sneakily from all sides. Finally, the More army was defeated but he saw that those 100 Mawale were still trying to defeat that amazing and brave soldier from More army. He was still undefeated and fighting the battle single handedly. Shivaji was not only brave but he also respected the brave people, even if they were fighting as his enemy. Shivaji went near that brave soldier and asked him his name. He was none other than Murarbaji. Shivaji asked him if he would join him in the fight for Swarajya. From that day Murarbaji joined Shivaji and became his trusted advisor.

When Shivaji won Purandar Fort, Shivaji made Netoji Palkar the fort keeper of Purandar and when Netoji became Sarnobaut, Shivaji made Murarbaji fort keeper of Purandar Fort.

Chapter 6

Veer Baji Jedhe

Fateh Khan was camping near Belasar. Belsar was near Purandar Fort. Shivaji knew that if he went to Purandar, we would be able to attack more easily. Also if Fateh Khan would have marched to Rajgad Fort, he would definitely have killed people or burnt houses.

Shivaji took his soldiers and went to Purandar Fort. The fort keeper of Purandar Fort was Mahadaji Sarnaik, a soldier of Bajpur and a trusted friend of Shahaji. Shivaji asked Sarnaik to help him. He opened the doors of the fort and let them in.

Then one day, Fateh Khan decided to win Subhanmangal Fort. The fort keeper fought his best but he lost to Fateh Khan. Shivaji was planning to attack Fateh Khan but then he got the news that he lost Subhanmangal fort. He picked his best 1,000 soldiers and captured the fort. Then Shivaji planned how to attack Fateh Khan. He decided to attack from the jungle. Shivaji made two groups. One team was carrying the saffron flag and the other was not holding a saffron flag. They sneakily went through the jungle and caught Fateh Khan's army by surprise. Fateh Khan's soldiers were shocked and ran helter skelter. Fateh Khan readied his army and said, "My soldiers, attack!" The Bajpur soldiers attacked. The other team of Marathas attacked and surrounded the enemy. Fateh Khan told his soldiers to go out of the Maratha formation. Fateh Khan's soldiers went out of the formation. They kept some soldiers fighting with the first team and surrounded the other team which was holding the saffron flag. The enemy killed the Maratha who was holding the flag. A brave soldier took his horse and rode to the Bijapurkar who was holding the saffron flag. The soldier took the flag and came back on the Maratha side. He gave the flag to another soldier, Fateh Khan was impressed by the soldier's bravery and said, "O brave soldier. What is your name?" The soldier looked at Fateh Khan and said, "My name is Baji Jedhe and I am just an humble soldier fighting for Shivaji Maharaj." Fateh Khan was surprised and ordered his soldiers to capture the flag which the soldier was holding. The Bijajpurkars surrounded the Maratha who was holding the flag. They killed him. The flag was about to fall but Bijapurkar picked it up. Then something as fast as light passed them. They looked at their hands and the Maratha flag was gone. They saw that the thing that had passed them by the speed of light was Baji Jedhe. He had grabbed the flag and had ridden away. The Baijapurkar who was holding the flag was dead. The Maratha soldiers surrounded Baji. With a sword in one hand, Baji started swinging it skillfully. Baji and his soldiers defeated Fateh Khan's soldiers who were surrounding the Marathas. The Marathas started retreating slowly. Then when they were far enough, they ran away. Shivaji was happy with Baji and rewarded him. He also changed his name from Baji Jedhe to Sarjerao Jedhe.

Thanks to Baji's bravery, the great saffron flag was saved.

Chapter 7

Shivaji defeats Fateh Khan.

A dil Shah had arrested Shahaji Raje because Shivaji captured his forts. He sent Fateh Jang Khan to capture Shivaji and stop him from winning more forts. When Fateh Jang Khan reached, he started climbing Purandar Fort. Shivaji's army started fighting Fateh Khan. They started throwing rocks from the top of the fort. Fateh Khan's army had no choice but to move backward. They were not able to fight Shivaji's army. Fateh Khan was thinking of how to fight Shivaji . He got an idea. He picked his best 100 soldiers and said, "We need to capture Shivaji. Once we put ladders on Purandar, we will quickly climb up and let the others climb." Their army followed his plan. The soldiers went to the top of Purandar and put the ladders up. When the soldiers were climbing, the mawle shot arrows at the soldiers. The Adil Shahi soldiers were not able to climb. When Fateh Khan got the news he was mad. He said, "These Marathas! They ruin all our plans." Just then Shivaji sent Baji Pasalkar to defeat Fateh Khan. Baji Pasalkar was 60 years old but still he went because he wanted his king to be safe. Baji opened the gates and his soldiers came out. The soldiers of Baji Pasalkar were shouting, "HAR HAR MAHADEV" and Fateh Khan's army was shouting, "DEEN DEEN!!" Soon both armies started a really fierce battle. The brave Marathas fought for their king and protected the fort.

Shivaji's soldiers won the battle and seeing this Fateh Khan ran for his life. Even after winning the battle, Baji Pasalkar wanted to capture FatehKhan. He along with Kawaji Malhar started chasing Fateh Khan. Both of them fought a heroic battle with Fateh Khan's army with all their might. Unfortunately, Fateh Khan escaped and the Marathas had to lose one of their brave soldiers. Baji Pasalkar lost his life fighting for the great cause of Swarajya.

The Badshah had learned his lesson and released Shahaji. The Badshah was furious about this defeat. He challenged all his sardars to capture Shivaji. Afzal Khan took oath to capture Shivaji and came to Maharashtra with 30,000 army. 20,000 people on foot 7,000 cavalry and 3,000 elephants. Afzal Khan was a serious danger to Swarajya and he was moving slowly towards Maharashtra. Marathi Swarajya was about to face one of the greatest dangers in history.

Chapter 8

Afzal Khan gets tricked.

A fzal Khan finally reached Maharashtra. Afzal Khan was troubling Maharashtra a lot. Afzal Khan stayed in Maharashtra and surrounded the villages. He started troubling the villagers. Shivaji got the message and decided to face Afzal Khan head on. But it was difficult to defeat Afzal Khan in an open battle since he had a big army. Shivaji decided to use guerilla warfare. Shivaji told Afzal Khan that he was ready to surrender and requested him to arrange a meeting so that they could discuss the next steps. Afzal Khan was delighted after hearing this news. They decided to meet in the middle of Pratapgadh Fort. Shivaji built a big tent there. Afzal Khan was told to bring only ten bodyguards. The Khan was so sure of his victory he brought only one bodyguard called Syed Banda close to the tent. Shivaji came with

Jiva Mahala and other ten bodyguards and wearing an armour on his head and chest and wore tiger claws and also put 2,000 soldiers in the jungle of Jawli. Those soldiers were hiding in the dense jungle, nobody even noticed them.

Afzal Khan was strong and tall. In comparison, Shivaji looked small in front of the tall Afzal Khan. Afzal Khan greeted Shivaji and came forward to give Shivaji a hug. Afzal Khan had an ulterior motive. He was very cunning and was planning to kill Shivaji. When Shivaji hugged Afzal Khan, Afzal Khan took his sword and banged it on Shivaji's head. The force broke the armour and gave a wound to Shivaji. But Shivaji was very quick on his feet and extremely alert. He immediately took the tiger claws out and pierced them in Afzal Khan's stomach. 'BETRAYAL' Shouted the Khan and died within a few seconds.. Syed Banda came inside the tent but before he realized what was happening Jiva Mahala cut his head and then cut Afzal Khan's head. He sent the head to Maa Saheb and buried it. Tanaji, Suryaji Malusare, Suryaji Kakte, Ramoji Pangera, Baji Jedhe, Netoji Palkar, Kudtoji Gujar, and other soldiers came out of the bushes. Shivaji made three groups and sent them to win as much as they could. In Shivaji's group, there was a man named Bandal.

Shivaji knew that they would not be able to pass unless they defeated Afzal Khan's soldiers. Shivaji sent some soldiers in the jungle to go down and then when they went, Shivaji started descending the hill slowly. Shivaji sat on his horse and went to Afzal Khan's army. He sent his troops everywhere and made Afzal Khan's soldiers chase them in the jungle. Shivaji already had his troops hiding in the jungle. With the help of his brave soldiers, Shivaji and his soldiers fought the battle skillfully. Then they used guerilla warfare and defeated Afzal Khan's soldiers. Without their leader, Afzal Khan's army could not sustain the attacks from Maratha soldiers. They surrendered in no time. Shivaji won 10,000 Hon (Currency in Shivaji's time), 10 elephants,

100 cannons, 20,000 camels, 1,000 soldiers and 2,000 cavalry. They also got a trustful soldier named Siddi Hillal. Shivaji left all that wealth on Pratapgad Fort. This unbelievable mission happened on November 10, 1659. Then Shivaji also went on to win Vishalgad Fort and Panhala Fort with the soldiers of Bandal.

But he did not get much time to celebrate this huge victory. There was another danger looming for Swarajya. The name of this danger was Siddi Jauhar.

Chapter 9

Baji Prabhu Deshpande.

It had been 18 days since the death of Afzal Khan and Shivaji and Netoji Palkar started conquering forts non-stop. Bandal helped Shivaji win Panhala Fort. Baji Prabhu Deshpande was a brave soldier from Bandal's army. He was a great warrior.

One day Adil Shah sent Siddi Jauhar to kill Shivaji. At that time Shivaji was in Miraj. When he heard about Siddi Jauhar, he immediately went to Panhala Fort. Siddi Jauhar followed him to Panhala Fort. He had to be stopped before he could destroy the area near Panhala Fort. When Siddi arrived, Shivaji fired the cannons and they had to turn back and set up tents where the cannons could not reach. Siddi along with his army surrounded the entire Panhala Fort. They set their tents around the fort. It had been 2 months but they hadn't left. Then the monsoon rain started. It was becoming hard to feed people in the fort. There was no way for the Maratha army to get their food and other necessary things up on the fort. Eventually Shivaji had to surrender. Shivaji sent a message to Siddi that he would be surrendering shortly. Siddi was really happy. All the guards of Siddi Jauhar began to rest and they were not as alert as they used to be. Later in the night Shivaji left the fort and fled to Vishalgad. Some of Siddi's soldiers saw them and rushed to inform Siddi. Siddi sent some soldiers to chase Shivaji. Shivaji had now reached Ghodkhind. Baji Prabhu told Shivaji that he would fight in Ghodkhind and defeat the army.

The Marathas started throwing rocks at Siddi's army which arrived in Ghodkhind. Then Baji came forward and started fighting by swinging his swords. Siddi's soldiers said to Baji, "Oh, you are a great soldier. Move aside !! If you don't, we'll kill you." Baji said, "Do whatever you want but I will never stop till Raje reaches Vishalgad. I will not let you all pass this Ghodkhind." Siddi's army went crazy. Siddi Masood asked Bajpurkar, "Who is this Baji?" The Sardar said, "The one in the middle who is covered in blood." Siddi Masood took a gun and fired at Baji. Baji Prabhu drew his sword without worrying about his life or without worrying about what would happen to him if the bullet hit him. Siddi Masood also saw this. He was impressed with Baji but because of him, he was not able to move forward. He tried to shoot another bullet at Baji's chest but Baji Prabhu extended his hand and the bullet hit his hand. Baji screamed in pain. Baji's army came to his aid. Baji said to the soldiers, "Let me fight. I will fight till Maharaj reaches Vishalgad". Baji fought for 9 hours. Baji was bathed in blood when he heard the sound of the cannon fired from Vishalgad. It was the sign that Shivaji Maharaj had reached safely on Vishalgad Fort. Baji felt relieved that Raje reached safely. For the last time he did a namaskar to Shivaji and he stopped fighting. Siddi Masood again shot him in the chest and Baji Prabhu Deshpande fell to ground. He died fighting for Shivaji. He sacrificed his life so that Shivaji Maharaj could be safe. His blood covered face had a different kind of satisfaction. The Marathas slowly started retreating. This happened on July 14, 1660.

When Shivaji heard this news, he felt really bad. He lost a great warrior. He honored the sacrifice of Baji Prabhu by building a statue of him. After this incident, the Ghodkhind was renamed as Pawankhind.

Chapter 10

Battle of Umberkhind.

Shahistya Khan had come to Pune but did not even try to attack. He sent Raibaghan and Kartalab Khan to win an area near Umberkhind. Kartalab Khan came near the fort named Lohagad. He tried winning the fort. He fired so many cannons that the fort was almost destroyed. The Marathas had to surrender the fort. Kartalab Khan now went ahead. There were two routes. Kartalab Khan took the route which led to Umberkhind.

In Rajgad, Shivaji said to Jijamata "Thank god Kartalab Khan took the route which our soldiers are on. Shivaji got the news that Kartalab Khan was about 10 miles away from Umberkhind. He, Netoji palkar, Tanaji, and Suryaji decided to attack. Everyone took 1,000 soldiers.

Shivaji and Tanaji hid behind a rock in Umberkhind. Suryaji and Netoji surrounded Umberkhind by hiding in the jungle. They kept a route for Kartalab Khan to come in. Soon, the chants of Deen Deen were heard. This was the moment the Marathas were waiting for. Shivaji shouted, "Get ready my Marathas!"

Soon, the first row of Mughals entered the khind. Slowly and steadily, the whole army came inside the valley of Umberkhind. The Marathas started blowing horns very loudly. The Mughals were surprised. The elephants started making chaos. Shivaji took a bow and arrow and aimed three arrows at the elephant Kartalab Khan was sitting on. He shot three arrows and defeated the elephant. Kartalab Khan got off his elephant and climbed on a horse and started fighting. He had one bow and arrow. Shivaji's soldiers started coming from both sides. The Khan's soldiers were really scared. Just then Tanaji dropped a big ball which was filled with honey bees in it. Suryaji took his bow and arrow and aimed it at the ball. Suryaji let the arrow go and it burst the ball. The honey bees caused chaos with the Mughal soldiers. Finally, the honey bees flew away. Shivaji came down and started a big fight. Chants of "Har Har Mahadev" filled the area. The Marathas were fighting too well. The Marathas were not worried about the moves. They were only trying to keep the Mughals fighting for a long time. The Mughals ran out of options to fight the Maratha army. They were trapped in a very narrow path of Umberkhind and surrounded by the Maratha army. Finally Raibaghan had to surrender but Kartalab Khan was not ready to surrender. Raibaghan told Karatlab Khan that if we kept fighting none of them would be alive and Shahistya Khan would lose. Kartalab Khan sent one of his soldiers to tell Shivaji. The soldier told Shivaji that he was a friend of Shahaji Raje and to please let them surrender. Shivaji let them surrender. The troops went to Kartalab Khan and then they turned back and went back to Shaistya Khan. Shaistya Khan was mad and sent them back to Delhi because he was not happy with them. This happened on 3 February 1661 The battle of Umberkhind gave the Marathas much needed confidence and energy to fight for Swarajya.

Chapter 11

Shahistya Khan won Sangram Durg.

S haistya Khan was angry because of the defeat of Umberkhind. He decided to attack the fort Sangram Durg and win it. He took his army and went to attack. The fort Sangram Durg was a Bhuikot fort. Bhuikot means it is a fort on land but it has very strong walls.

Firangoji Narsala was on the fort. Firangoji Narsala and his men threw rocks on the Mughals. Shahistsya Khan was walking around the fort looking for a way to win the fort. Shaistya Khan was not just powerful but he was also smart and cunning.

He used cannons to try to break the walls but Sangram Durg's walls were so strong that it did not work. The Marathas repulsed the attack by copying them. The Marathas were safe but the Mughals were facing terrible defeat. The Marathas showered arrows which were on fire and burnt the Mughal tents. The Mughals had to handle that.

Shahistya Khan then decided to put ladders to climb. The Marathas let them put the ladders and then when the people started climbing, the Marathas started shooting arrows. They cut every single ladder and the Mughals fell down.

Shahistya Khan decided to win the fort no matter what. He picked the best 1,000 people and told them to climb the fort without ladders and then open the doors of the fort. The Mughals somehow made it up but the Marathas fired so many cannons on the Mughals that the Mughals were dying very quickly. The 1,000 people were fighting and while fighting, 900 Mughals died. So the 100 Mughals jumped down the fort. Even this attempt failed.

Shahistya Khan was mad. He gave shovels to his soldiers to dig a small underground tunnel towards the buruj (bastion) of the fort. The Marathas did not know that. When it was done, Shahistya Khan placed huge explosives and aimed an arrow at the explosives. Shahistya Khan let the arrow go and stepped 30 feet away. The explosion made a huge sound. The Mughals were thrown off their feet. Because of the explosion, the other explosives also exploded. One of the buruj(bastion) on Sangram Durg fell and the Mughals went inside the fort.

The Marathas tried putting up a big fight. Firangoji made sure no one came from the outside to give support to Shahistya Khan's army so he was fighting near the door of the fort. Then the Mughals dug a tunnel to the door of Sangram Durg and then they lit the explosives on fire. Firangoji saw the Mughals were standing far from the door so he knew they were trying to explode the door of Sangram Durg. He noticed the Mughals were fighting near the door before but now they were staying far away. Firangoji ran to the other side. Due to explosion, door became weak but it did not fall. Shahistya Khan used an elephant to ram the. The door fell and the Mughals poured into the fort.

Now the Marathas were fighting for a fort which was almost destroyed. They fought for so long but finally, that fort was lost. The Marathas fought bravely till the last minute but they could not sustain in front of Shahistya Khan's big army and his determination to win the fort. The Marathas now ran away in the huge crowd and wrote a letter to Shivaji. They told Shivaji that Sangram Durg was lost. They told Shivaji that they put up a huge fight but they had no choice but to accept the defeat. Shivaji sent a letter back boosting their morale. He said, "It is ok. You tried and gave a good fight. I am proud of your bravery. We will win that fort back. This incident took place in 1660. After this defeat, Firangoji then went to Bhupalgad Fort.

Chapter 12

Shahistya Khan

Shahistya Khan was still in Maharashtra. He was still a danger to Swarajya. Shahistya Khan was living in Pune for more than two years. He was living in Lal Mahal. Shivaji was really mad about it. Shivaji wanted to get rid of Shahistya Khan. He was trying to figure out ways to defeat Shahistya Khan.

One day, Shivaji disguised himself as a Mughal. He took only 60 soldiers with him. They tricked the guards. When Shivaji reached the palace, it was very dark. Shivaji took off his disguise and went in towards Shahistya Khan's chamber. He encountered one of Shahistya Khan's wives. The Marathas thought that she was a soldier because they could not see in the dark. She was killed by the Marathas. When they came into the chamber Shahistya Khan was asleep. Shahistya Khan's bodyguards realized what was happening and they tried to fight but they were killed in a second. Shahistya Khan woke up because of the sound and then he saw 20 Marathas surrounding him. Shahistya Khan tried to jump out of the window. Shivaji saw him jumping and ran to him. In a swift strike of his sword, he cut off Shahistya Khan's fingers. The Maraths opened the doors of the palace. They were still disguised as the Mughals. They started shouting, "Enemy, Enemy." There was chaos everywhere. The Marathas took advantage of this chaos and swiftly got out of the palace without anybody's notice. This shocking incident happened on 5th of April 1663. In the attack, 2 nephews of Shahistya Khan, 1 wife, 100 soldiers, and 1 of his sons were killed.

Just imagine the risk Shivaji was taking here. He went inside the enemy's camp himself. It was full of enemy soldiers. There were soldiers every step of the way and he took only 60 Marathas with him. He was a true leader, the one who fought the battle with his men shoulder to shoulder. That is the reason Shivaji was not only a great king but he was a great warrior, a great leader and a pioneer in the true sense.

Chapter 13

Looting of Surat.

Shivaji had lost a lot of money in the wars and now Jaswant Singh had surrounded Kondhana. Shivaji needed money to keep fighting for Swarajya. He needed money to repair the forts which were destroyed by the Mughals. Surat was ruled by Aurangzeb. It was one of the richest cities in India. Shivaji's spies were already living in Surat. They told Shivaji about the merchants who were rich and loyal to Aurangzeb. Shivaji decided to loot Surat to get money from those merchants. At night Shivaji quietly traveled to loot Surat. It took 4 - 5 days to reach Surat. He asked everyone to gather and asked the rich merchants to give some money for Swarajya. He did not even touch the house of those who gave money but whoever did not would have their money looted by the Maratha army. The main Subhedar of Surat told his soldiers to kill Shivaji. They went to Shivaji's tent and started talking to Shivaji. Suddenly one of the soldiers said, "Oh look at this Shivaji. So young." The Marathas were mad but before they could do anything, one of the Mughals took his knife and tried to put it in Shivaji's chest but Shivaji turned around and made the knife hit his hand. Shivaji's soldiers were now very mad. The Marathas took their swords and started striking their swords on the enemies. The Mughals that were left ran away. For four more days Shivaji looted Surat. Then Shivaji got the news that Mahabat Khan was coming to Surat and so he rode away. Then Shivaji used that money to build a fort named Sindhudurg.

Chapter 14

Shahaji Raje dies.

Shahaji Raje asked Adil Shah, "Can I go hunting?" Adil Shah said yes. "Shahaji Raje went with 10 bodyguards. While Shahaji Raje was going to the forest of Hodigrehen, he saw a tiger. He got on his horse and chased him. Shahaji hunted the tiger and pitched his tent. The next day Shahaji Raje went hunting again. He told his bodyguards to stay alert. Make sure every village around the forest is safe. That's when Shahaji Raje saw a deer. He decided to hunt it down. He chased after her with a horse. Suddenly, the horse's leg got stuck in a rock. Shahaji Raje fell down from the horse. Shahaji Raje fell on his face and was hit hard. He realized that it was Bhavani Mata telling him to go back to Heaven. Shahaji Raje extended his hand and uttered his last words "I am coming. I am coming Bhavani Devi." He breathed his last breath shortly. Adil Shah felt very bad. He informed Shivaji about this sad news. Shivaji could not believe this. He was extremely sad and wished he could have done something to save his father. Shivaji made a small idol for Shahaji Raje. Even Shivaji's Mawle felt bad that Shivaji's father had died there. Shivaji was deeply overwhelmed with this shocking news. He had not met his father for 2 years. He lost a great support from his father. He lost a very kind, doting father who had also tried to free Pune once but failed. In the true sense, he was a brave soldier who motivated Shivaji to fight for Swarajya.

Chapter 15

Murarbaji

Shahistya Khan had been defeated. So Aurangzeb sent the commander in chief, Mirza Raje Jai Singh along with Diler Khan. Mirza Raje Jai Singh was very brave and had been a loyal soldier to Aurangzeb. He was well respected in the Mughal army as well as in the Maratha army. Diler Khan was brave and cunning just like Shahistya Khan.

They surrounded the fort Purandar for a long time. One day they decided to win Vajragad so they could come one step closer to winning Purandar Fort. The soldiers of Vajragad Fort fought very courageously but they lost.

The Mughsls tried to win Purandar Fort by firing the cannons from Vajragad Fort. But they were not successful. They tried other means to capture Purandar Fort but all their efforts went in vain.

Then Diler Khan decided to take 5,000 soldiers and attack Purandar head on but when Murarbaji found this out he took his best 700 soldiers. He started defending the fort with much less army but each mawala in the army was so brave and driven to defend the fort that Diler Khan was struggling to capture the fort. While Diler Khan and his soldiers were climbing the fort, Murarbaji made them move downwards by firing cannons on them. The Mughals were forced to stay at the bottom of the fort. Suddenly Diler Khan noticed that the door of Purandar was being opened. He then saw someone riding the horse down the mountain at full speed. It was none other than Murarbaji himself. There were many Marathas following him down the mountain. Diler Khan rushed to the battle. Before the Mughals even realized the gravity of the situation, they were already deep in the battle. The Mughal soldiers were dead on the rocks. The Maratha army was fighting the battle to protect their fort. Suddenly, Murarbaji was surrounded by the Mughals. Diler Khan thought that Murarbaji might be scared and would surrender but to his surprise, Murarbaji spurred his horse and rode speedily. Then he trampled the Mughals like ants. Diler Khan was sitting on his elephant. Diler Khan saw how well Murarbaji fought. He asked Murarbaji to join his army but Murarbaji denied without thinking even for a moment. He said, "Who are you to decide?" I only work for Shivaji Maharaj. Shivaji Raje is like a god to me and there is no way I will betray his trust." Diler Khan got mad and took his bow and arrow and shot it at Murarbaji's neck and Murarbaji died in a moment. The Maratha army noticed that their leader had fallen but they decided to keep on fighting. 20 Marathas came with a Palkhi and put Murarbaji in it. They carried it all the way to Purandar Fort. They informed the rest of the Maratha army at Purandar Fort and requested them to join the battle. 300 more Marathas rode into the battle. Diler Khan said, "Poor Marathas. You lost your commander." The Marathas said, "We may have lost our commander but we still have not lost our courage." Then the Marathas started fighting again, this time for the honor of their brave commander. A lot of Diler Khan's Mughal army died but he had a lot many soldiers waiting to join the battle. The Marathas also lost many brave soldiers. There were many wounded soldiers too. But they showed unparalleled bravery to stop the attack on Purandar Fort. This battle went on for almost 4 months. There was extreme damage to Purandar Fort. There were a lot of lives lost on both sides.

When Shivaji heard about this, He took a very difficult decision to surrender Purandar Fort. The lives of his Maratha soldiers were much more important to him than the fort. He thought that he could win this fort again if he saved his brave soldiers from the great danger. He decided to see Mirza Raje Jai Singh and talk to him about stopping these attacks. He heard about the fierce battle which was going on at Purandar Fort. He could listen to all the cannon sounds continuously. He sent his trusted advisers Raghunath Pant and Prataprao Gujar to Purandar Fort. He asked them to tell all the people on the Fort Purandar to come down and surrender the fort. It was a hard decision but it had to be taken for the safety of his people. There were even more tough choices to be made.

Chapter 16

Mirza Raje Jaisingh and Shivaji meet.

When Shivaji went into Mirza Raje's tent, Mirza Raje was sitting on a huge couch. His bodyguards were tall and strong. Shivaji came with Yesaji Kank, Kondaji, Jiva Mahala, Suryaji Katke, Sambhaji Kavji, Krishnaji Gaikwad, Kataji Ingle, Sambhaji Karvar and Yesaji Murumbak. Mirza Raje had 10 bodyguards. Shivaji sat on another couch. The Mughals were looking at Shivaji with high interest. Mirza Raje ordered his soldiers to bring a sword for Shivaji.

Mirza Raje gave the sword to Shivaji. Shivaji accepted it. Shivaji heard the cannons from Vajragad Fort crashing on Purandar Fort. He was very much concerned about the safety of his soldiers. Shivaji requested Mirza Raje Jai Singh, "Please stop this attack. I will surrender Purandar Fort." Mirza Raje knew that this opportunity would not present itself again. If he didn't take advantage of this now, Shivaji would never be trapped like this again. So, Mirza Raje asked Shivaji to surrender not only Purandar Fort but all his forts. Shivaji was not only a great warrior but a great leader. He negotiated with Mirza Raje for 3 days. He finally had to agree to surrender 23 forts. Mirza Raje was delighted to hear this. Aurangzeb sent so many of his commanders to defeat Shivaji but no one was able to achieve such a spectacular victory. He told Shivaji that, "It is Badshah's 50th birthday. Why don't you go to Agra and meet him?" Shivaji trusted Mirza Raje and agreed to go to Agra. Shivaji asked Mirza Raje to promise him the safety of him and Shambhu Raje in Agra. Mirze Raje agreed to protect them both in Agra. Shivaji had another question. He said, "Why don't you challenge Aurangzeb for the throne?" Mirza Raje had no answer to give.

The next day Shivaji met the leader of the artillery. The leader was an Italian person named Niccolao Manucci. Niccolao Manucci wrote a book named Moghul India. In that book he wrote about the Mughals. Niccolao Manucci had travelled at the age of twelve to find a job. His boat landed in Goa. That time, Mirza Raje was there. He met Niccolao and asked him if he would work for him. Niccolao Manucci started working for Mirza Raje.

Shivaji met him and shook his hand. They talked about many things. Then Niccolao Manucci asked, "How are only a few Marathas able to beat the Mughals into a pulp?" Shivaji laughed. He said, "I have many trusted friends who are motivated by a common cause. We want to establish the kingdom of our own people. We want to create a kingdom where everyone feels safe and secure. We know that it is hard to defeat Aurangzeb's army in an open battle so we use Guerilla warfare. We know our land well so we can take advantage of that knowledge.

As per the conditions of peace talks, Shivaji joined the Mughals to win karnataka. He fought alongside the Mughals but he did not win that battle. He failed on purpose because he did not want the Mughals getting a bigger kingdom.

Admitting to Mirza Raje's demands was one of the hardest decisions that Shivaji took in his life. He had to sacrifice 23 forts which he along with his army earned with vigorous fight. But there were many more great battles to be fought in the future.

Chapter 17

Escape from Agra.

S hivaji went to Agra and met Aurangzeb. Aurangzeb did not treat Shivaji with respect. He did not give him the deserved honor and respect. Shivaji was not happy with this. He refused to visit Aurangzeb's court. Aurangzeb considered this as a dishonor. Aurangzeb did not want Shivaji to go back to Maharashtra and start the fight again. Aurangzeb thought that Shivaji had some kind of plan to escape. Aurangzeb ordered Radandaz Khan to keep a close eye on Shivaji. Shivaji kept visiting the big sardars' homes. One day, when he went to the wazir's house he said to the wazir, "Please ask Aurangzeb to let me go. I will give my entire army and Swaraj. I will also become his Mansabdar. I too will fight in every battle." The wazir said, "First give us the money and Swaraj, then we shall see about you." Shivaji then sent a letter to Aurangzeb. It said, "Please let me go. I will give my entire army and Swarajya. I will also become your Mansabdar. I will also fight in every battle." Aurangzeb answered "I do not allow you to leave. I have planned a fight against the Afghan kings. You help me in that battle. After the fight, you can go home." Shivaji knew that if this happens, while he was fighting, RadandazKhan could sneak up and cut his head off. Then he would tell the mawle that Shivaji died while fighting. He told Aurangzeb that Mirza Raje told him that nothing would happen to him. Aurangzeb sent a letter to Mirza Raje. He wrote, "Why did you tell Shivaji that he would not die in Agra? This is what I sent you there for. Come back to Agra now!" Aurangzeb was really mad at this situation. He decided to put Shivaji under house arrest. He prohibited Shivaji from meeting anyone. It took a month for Mirza Raje's answer to come. It said, "What promise? I only promised Shivaji about the forts and his mother and army." Aurangzeb was mad. Shivaji knew that now he was in big trouble. He started plotting a plan to escape from Agra. Shivaji gathered his friends around him. Hiroji Farzand, Ragho Mitra Sarjerao, Manakoji, and others. Shivaji was thinking about his escape. He spread a rumor about his ill health. He started telling everyone that he is sick and has very few days left to live. He wanted to donate food to the poor during his last days. He decided to give boxes of sweets everyday. Everyday the guards were checking baskets. Day after day the guards kept on checking the boxes of sweets. They now were bored of doing the same job and stopped checking every single box. Shivaji took advantage of their ignorance. One day Shivaji climbed in the box. Hiroji Farzand pretended to be Shivaji and stayed behind in the cell so that no one suspected Shivaji's escape. The box was carried outside the tent. Later even Hiroji escaped from the tent. When Auranzeb realized that Shivaji escaped the tent, he punished the guards and sent his army everywhere to look for Shivaji. But Shivaji was long gone. In a lonely spot Shivaji got out of the box and climbed on his horse with Sambhaji and rode away.

This was the great escape and no easy feat.

Chapter 18

Attack on Portugese army.

S hivaji declared truce with the Bijapurkar army and the Mughals. Shivaji decided to launch an attack on the Portugese in Goa. Shivaji readied his army. They took 20,000 men. The Portugese opened the doors of their castle and came to fight. Shouts of "Legionários, quem vive" were in the air. The Marathas were shouting, "Shivaji maharaj ki jai!" Both armies clashed. Spears,cannonballs, and swords were laying all around. Shivaji sat in his chariot and started fighting with his bow and arrow. They had a huge battle but Shivaji's army was not able to secure Goa.

Shivaji decided to put ladders to the fort and climb up. The Marathas tried to climb up but they couldn't. Shivaji tried many other things but that did not work. Shivaji had to surrender and turn back. He left a 200 strong army in Goa so he could plan another attack but a spy from Goa found this and captured those 200 people. He told the leader of the Portugese about it. Those men were captured. Shivaji felt bad about this defeat but he thought about this calmly. He decided to fight this battle later. He wanted to win Goa but he decided to focus on Janjira Fort first.

Chapter 19

Janjira Fort

S hivaji decided to focus his attention on winning Janjira fort. This castle was very tough. You could fit 1,200 cannons in it. There was one very big cannon.

Only one army was able to win it. The army was of a fisherman. Their king was named Koli Raja. He was ruling the fort Janjira.

Siddi wanted to win that fort. But it was a very difficult fort to win in a direct battle. He decided to use a trick to win the fort from Koli Raja. Siddi's people came to the fort to give food to people on the fort. They started coming to the fort regularly to deliver the food. One day, they brought around 1300 baskets of food. But only 100 baskets contained food, the rest of the baskets had soldiers hiding in them. It was really tough to win Janjira with only 1,200 soldiers but they were able to win the fort. Now, Siddi had taken over the Janjira Fort by defeating Koli Raja.

Then Mohhamad Adil Shah sent his soldiers to defeat him and win Janjira. He was not able to. Then the fort keeper of Janjira won the fort back. From that time Shivaji knew it was impossible to win Janjira. Shivaji surrounded Janjira for about 4 months. Nothing happened. Shivaji thought that when they ran out of food they would fight him. But then Siddi Fateh Khan decided to hand over the fort. Four Siddis got mad. They put their master in jail and ruled Janjira. They sent a letter to Aurangzeb which said, "You are a very strong Badshah. Shivaji is troubling us. We need your help. If you help, Janjira will be yours." A Siddi soldier was ordered to sneak out past the surrounding army and ??. At that time, Bahirji Naik was in the court of Aurangzeb when the letter arrived. Bahirji Naik informed Shivaji about this. Shivaji immediately stopped the siege of Janjira and went back to the Swarjya's safety and the three year truce.

Chapter 20

Sambhaji and Shah Alam.

S hivaji needed some money to take care of his kingdom. He was thinking of ways to get the money. Then he remembered that Aurangzeb was going to give Shambhu Raje a Jahagir of a village near Aurangabad with 5,000 soldiers. Shivaji sent a letter to Aurangzeb. It said, "Please give Shambhu Raje his Jahagir. I will be king of Maharashtra but you will be my overlord." After 20 days he got his answer. Auranzeb had sent a letter which said, "I accept it. Shambhu Raje will meet my son Shah Alam/Shazzada Moazzam/ Akbar ll." Aurangzeb did not actually want to say yes but he did not want Shivaji to start fighting him in Maharashtra. Sambhaji went to meet the Mughal prince. The Mughal prince did not like to fight the battles. He was only interested in getting the throne but he never really wanted to go on any mission. He did not like how cruel his father was. He was like Akbar or Darashuko. He gave Sambhaji 5,000 soldiers, one elephant, 50 cannons, 1,000 rupees,and a sword. When Sambhaji returned to Rajgad, he gave Shivaji 3,000 of the soldiers, cannons and the money. Shivaji used this to build a big army. The peace agreement with Aurangzeb lasted for 3 years. Shivaji focused on making his Swarajya strong. He worked on many projects to help his people. This peace agreement gave him a chance to work on building roads, forming a proper tax system.

Chapter 21

Tanaji Malusare

Shivaji really wanted Kondhana to be in his kingdom but he knew it was impossible to win. At Rajgad, he asked his soldiers, "Who will win the Kondhana fort for me?" A soldier named Tanaji Malusare said that he would do this but Shivaji could not let him go because his son Raiba was getting married. Tanaji said that before he attended his son's wedding he would win Kondhana. Shivaji felt bad and did not want Tanaji to go on such a risky mission. But Tanaji told Shivaji that he would not even show his face unless he won Kondhana. Shivaji agreed to let Tanaji go on this dangerous mission with a heavy heart.

Kondhana's fort keeper was a Rajput named Udaybhan. Shivaji was waiting at Rajgad for the news about Tanaji winning the fort. He walked up to Jijamata. She was also awake. Shivaji said, "Why are you awake Maa saheb?" Jijamata said, "How can I sleep when our men are fighting in Kondhana?" Shivaji walked back to the area where he could see Kondhana and said to his bodyguard, "In my mind, I have a battle going on." Then Shivaji saw flames rising on Kondhana. This meant Kondhana was won by the Marathas.

Shivaji rode to Kondhana. He saw Tanaji laying on the rocks. Shivaji asked a soldier, "What happened to Tanaji? The soldiers said, "Tanaji came with his best 700 soldiers. Suryaji hid near the Kalyan gate with his 500 brave soldiers. Tanaji released a ghorpad (a monitor lizard) on a rock and the lizard started climbing. When they reached the top. Tanaji went to the head and tied the rope to a large rock. He threw down a lot of ropes. Some of Udaybhan's soldiers saw them. The soldiers that had already arrived began to fight to prevent the ropes from breaking. A rope was cut and a few mawle fell down and died. The other soldiers began to advance rapidly. A fierce battle ensued. When Udaybhan heard the news, he rushed to Tanaji. He broke Tanaji's shield but Tanaji did not stop. Tanaji knew that if he would have stopped to take the shield of a nearby dead man, Udayabhan would have cut off his head. They both were fighting with all their power. It was like two lions fighting. Tanaji used his left hand as a shield and attacked with his right hand. Then his hand was cut off but he didn't care. Tanaji was struck with swords everywhere. The Mawle also fought so well that 1,000 soldiers died before the enemy was ready. The main target was now Udaybhan. Tanaji raised his sword. In one fell swoop, he broke Udaybhan's shield and struck Udaybhan on the chest with the tip of his sword. Udaybhan and Tanaji jumped up. They took their swords and in one strike, they attacked each other so hard that Tanaji and Udaybhan got terribly injured. In this fierce fight, both Tanaji and Udaybhan died. The mawle saw this and began to flee. Meanwhile some mawle saw this and ran to open the Kalyan door. Suryaji saw this. Suryaji shouted at the Maratha army, "Are you worried about Tanaji or yourself?!! Remember. If you run away, Raje will not be pleased with you." The mawle were afraid to die but they did not want to let Shivaji down. They had only one option: fight. They turned and started attacking again. Udaybhan's army fled and finally, we had conquered Kondhana. Shivaji was sad to lose Tanaji. He was not only a soldier to him but he was also his childhood friend, his trusted advisor and great warrior. He made a monument for Tanaji on Kondhana. Suryaji was made the chief of Kondhana and Raiba the chief of Pargad. People say that Kondhana got the name Sinhagad because of Tanaji. Shivaji asked Nilopant to further strengthen the fort. Shivaji thought it was really impossible to climb the fort so he named it Sinhagad because it was as strong as a lion. But Tanaji did something impossible, he climbed the impossible mountain. Shivaji later built a wall there to secure the entry to Kondhana/Sinhagad. Tanaji's bravery was remembered for ages.

Chapter 22

Battle of Salher.

Bahadur Khan had surrounded Salher and Malher fort with 12,000 army. Suddenly they got a rough attack from Prataprao Gujar and 5,000 soldiers. Prataprao sent some Marathas to fight and kept some with him. Bahadur Khan's soldiers were in a plain area but the Maratha soldiers were fighting so good that there were no match for Maratha soldiers. Prataprao was sitting on a horse with a sword in his hand. Prataprao shouted "Attack!" The Marathas attacked. In the middle of battle, Prataprao Gujar and his army retreated to a nearby khind. Not knowing it was a trick, the Mughal soldiers followed them. Anandrao Makaji was hiding in the trees near khind with another 5,000 soldiers. They surrounded the army. Anandrao penetrated Bahadur Khan's soldiers. Prataprao also did the same. Suryaji Kakade, a friend of Shivaji, was fighting really skillfully. The camels in Bahadur Khan's army started running away. The Marathas started moving back. They came out of the khind. The Mughals followed them. Suryaji Kakade went in front of the enemy and started fighting. The Marathas also came up to fight. The Marathas fought for some more time and then ended the battle. They defeated Bahadur Khan. In the fight Suryaji kakte's bravery was unparalleled. He was hit by a cannonball from the Zamburak cannon during the fight but he still kept fighting till the battle was won.

Chapter 23

Second attack on Surat.

Mirza Raje had taken all the loot Shivaji had got from Surat. Shivaji needed money for his kingdom. He decided to attack Surat one more time. English spies found this out. They wrote a letter to the English soldiers in Surat to be careful. They also suggested to hide and shoot bullets if they encounter any attack from the Marathas. Streynsham master, an English officer, got the news. He had only Fifty soldiers and Shivaji had about Eighteen Thousand. Shivaji got the news that the Streynsham master was waiting. Shivaji came and waited 9 kilometers away from Surat. He did not enter Surat for the next three days. The English soldiers were still on their guard. The next day, Shivaji sent Ten thousand men to loot Surat. The moment

The Marathas came in, the English soldiers shot bullets. They were shooting with very much speed. The Marathas were falling quickly. They had to retreat. But they decided to regroup and attack again after a few days.

In a few days, the Marathas got the news that a Sultan from Afghanistan had come to Surat. He was very rich and had a bed made out of gold. The Marathas planned an attack on him. The Marathas went to where the Sultan was coming. They had a big battle. The Sultan was pushed into the Surats fort and was locked in. The Marathas took the bed to Maharaj. They broke the bed and got the gold.

The Marathas then went on to fight English soldiers. They still had a big battle. The English lost 25 men and the Marathas had lost about 500. The Marathas asked the English soldiers to give Raje a gift or he would take all his 40,000 men and finish all the English soldiers. The English agreed and gave them 100,000 Rupees.

Shivaji even fought with the Dutch to secure weaponry. The Dutch gave Shivaji cannonballs.

Shivaji managed to get 8 Million Rupees in the loot. All this loot was now being used to build a better Swarajya for all the common people.

Chapter 24

Battle of Dindori.

Aurangzeb kept on sending different Sardars from his court to capture Shivaji. The Sardar who Aurangzeb sent to stop Shivaji from getting the loot was really slow. He went 5 miles a day. Finally he reached the state Shivaji was in. He sent half of his army to search Shivaji. If they went where Shivaji was, the Marathas chased them away. The Mughal sardar realized that it is not easy to capture Shivaji. He turned away and left for Delhi.

Aurangzeb thought of Mirza Raje. He was not able to stop Shivaji from taking the loot but he was able to make Shivaji return the loot the first time. But Auranzeb did send Mirza Raje this time instead he wanted to send his fastest Sardar who was always on the run. He thought of Diler Khan but Diler Khan had barely 20,000 soldiers and Shivaji had

50,000 soldiers. Aurangzeb finally decided to send IkhlasKhan and Daud Khan.

While they were marching in Dindori, they were attacked by Shivaji's army. Shivaji sent away the loot with his few soldiers and stayed back in Dindori with 5,000 soldiers. He had Dandpatas in both hands. Ikhlas Khan told his army to come out and fight. The Mughals were busy wearing their armours. Shivaji took the opportunity and attacked. Ikhlas Khan and some of his army finally started fighting. Shivaji had attacked in such a battle form that once the Sardar came inside their formation, he would never go out. Ikhlas Khan entered the formation. The Marathas surrounded him. He took two swords in his hand. Then more of his soldiers joined him. He was swinging his swords very fast. Shivaji saw this. He came to fight. He and IkhalasKhan fought for 1 hour. Shivaji got many wounds but Ikhlas Khan got more. He struggled to fight. Then Daud Khan came and took Ikhlas Khan on his horse and rode away. He put IkhlasKan on the bed and came out to fight again. He sat on his elephant, took his bow and arrow, and started shooting. The Marathas had to knock him off. Yesaji came forward and knocked him off. Some Mughals made a bed for him so he would not fall. The Mughals were hurt but Daud Khan was saved. The Mughals started falling quickly. 8,000 Mughals died but 1,000 Mawle died and 2,000 were wounded. Daud Khan put Ikhlas Khan on his horse and rode away at his fastest speed.

Shivaji won the battle of Dindori with the help of his brave soldiers. It was a battle to remember.

Chapter 25

Shivaji wins Panhala from Siddi Jauhar.

It had been 10 years since Panhala was with the Bijapurkars army. Shivaji knew winning Panhala would be a difficult mission. He did not want to surround it with most of his army. He was aware that while he was busy with Panhala, Aurangzeb, Qutub Shah might attack his other forts.

There were two Subedars on Panhala. One was Bahlol Khan. Shivaji thought for some time. He was thinking of a strategy to win Panhala Fort. Moropant and Annajipant came in. They asked Shivaji, "Raje? What are you thinking about? If you say so should we help you?"

Shivaji shared what he was thinking about. Moropant laughed. He shared the solution. Shivaji was amazed. The difficult Panhala Fort mission was now looking like a possible mission.

He sent three thousand men to camp near Panhala. He knew a Sardar named Kondaji Pharjand, a very brave person who never stops fighting once he starts. Shivaji quickly called him. Kondaji did a Mujra and they discussed some plan and then Kondaji left.

The same day, Kondaji took his 60 brave men and left for Panhala Fort. At night they were chatting when a cannon boomed. The doors of Panhala were closing. They gathered up their men and walked around the mountain. They saw where there was no wall. They quietly went up the cliff with only 60 men. Kondaji raised his hand and said, "Jay Bhavani!" Firangoji took the drums and made a huge racket. The enemies got alert and ran because they thought it was Shivaji and his whole army had come to attack them. They were so scared that most of them ran away. Only a few stayed behind. Firangoji climbed up and threw big ropes. The Mawle climbed the fort using the rope. A big battle started. Kondaji started fighting with 50 people at a time. The enemy was about to cut a rope when Firangoji quietly went behind him and started tickling him. The enemy dropped his sword. Firangoji took the chance and put his sword through the Bijapurkars' soldiers. The Marathas came up and fought fiercely. When the Subedar got the news, he came and killed two Marathas. Kondaji rushed to him. Firangoji also came but a soldier came to kill Kondaji so he had to go to fight him. Kondaji put a wound on the Subedar. They fought for 1 hour. Both of them were tired. Kondaji quickly took his sword and cut the enemies hand. He died. Kondaji was happy and went to find Bahlol Khan. Bahlol quickly ran away. Panhala fort was won with not only power but with strategies.

Shivaji was very delighted to hear the news. He visited Panhala and gifted everyone with treats. Balaji was one of the 60 soldiers who fought bravely to win Panhala Fort. Shivaji gave Balaji 200 soldiers and a sword.

Shivaji always knew how to treat his soldiers with respect and equality. He never shied away from giving the credits to those who deserved.

Chapter 26

Bahlol Khan is captured.

Khavas Khan sent Bahlol Khan to win Maharashtra. He came in and began camping. He was going everywhere to win Maharashtra. Shivaji knew if this goes on, he will have to fight him forever. Shivaji called Prataprao immediately to the Darbar. He said to Prataprao, "If this goes on for long, our Maratha strength will be like mice drowned in a Tsunami. Do something. We need to find a way to stop Bahlol Khan before he gets too dangerous and start troubling the common people."

Prataprao sent his spies everywhere to find Bahlol Khan. Bahlol Khan was camping near Umrani. Prataprao got the news that everyday he goes to a river and bathes there. He informed Shivaji about his plan. Shivaji just reminded him.,"Remember that an Elephant is scared of mice even if it is a thousand times bigger. Just like that, even if we are less in number, we are brave and dedicated to our goal. My one brave soldier is enough to take down an entire army of Bahlol Khan." Prataprao nodded and went. The next day, Marathas hid near the river, waiting for Bahlol Khan. The Bajpur people started taking the elephants to the river to let them drink some water. With them, Thousands of people came without their swords and armour to bathe. The soldiers saw something near the river. The Elephants came near when dust flew. Out of the dust came 3 thousand Marathas. The Marathas went like a Tsunami killing all the soldiers of the enemy who were in the way. Prataprao was fighting at the front. Bahlol Khan noticed that the soldiers who went to take a bath did not come back for a long time. He sent some soldiers to find out why. When they were near the river they saw the giant Maratha army coming towards them. They ran and informed Bahlol Khan. Bahlol Khan got mad. He sent all his soldiers to fight. He led himself to the attack on a horse. The Marathas came close. They raised their swords and shouted, "Har Har Mahadev!" Prataprao and Bahlol Khan went face to face. Bahlol Khan took his sword and attacked the brave soldier. Prataprao got mad. He was about to kill Bahlol Khan when a bullet struck him. He fell off his horse. Prataprao still got up and started fighting again. The Marathas thought he was dead and started running. Prataprao saw this and shouted to the Marathas "Come back and fight!!" The Marathas saw this and turned back. The Marathas went into the enemy's army and looted an elephant. They held the elephant and ordered the mahout to bring the elephant on their side. The war lasted for a ½ day. Finally Bahlol Khan surrendered. Prataprao made a grave mistake and trusted the cunning Bahlol Khan. Instead of throwing him in jail or taking him to Shivaji, Prataprao let him go. Bahlol Khan promised Prataprao that he will never return to Maharashtra. Pratprao trusted him and allowed him to go. But he did not keep his promise. He never left Maharashtra instead he stayed in Kolhapur waiting for another opportunity to attack.

Chapter 27

Prataprao Gujar

After Senapati Netoji, Prataprao Gujar had become commander in chief. He had defeated Bahlol Khan but let him go. Also Ali Adil Shah had died. His son, a mere child, was crowned. He was very young so Khavas Khan took his place. Bahlol Khan requested Khavas Khan to allow him to take revenge for his defeat. He came back with 20,000 troops.

Shivaji was not happy with Prataprao Gujar. He knew that Bahlol Khan would return and this time with more troops. Shivaji sent a letter to Prataprao. It said, "Once the rains are over, Abdul Karim Bahlol Khan will return and this time with more troops. You should not have let him go. Now, do not show your face till you capture Bahlol Khan."

Before the rains ended, Prataprao Gujar and Moropant met. Prataprao Gujar said, "If we both close the English factory which is building and sending weapons in Maharashtra, Raje might be pleased with us." Moropant and Prataprao Gujar shut down the British factory but Raje still was not pleased. He could see the danger of Bahlol Khan over his Swarajya.

Prataprao sent a letter to Surat. It said, "You depend on Aurangzeb to protect you. We looted Surat 2 times and where was Aurangzeb? He did not even protect you. Give us half the tax you guys give Aurangzeb or we will take our whole army and loot the whole Surat." Surat started giving money to Shivaji but still he was not happy with Prataprao. Prataprao was not able to figure out a way to correct his mistake. He really wanted Raje to trust him again. But he was unsuccessful in all his attempt to do so.

Soon, the rains ended. Prataprao got the news Bahlol Khan is now again attacking villages. This time Prataprao did not want to leave any stone unturned to capture Bahlol Khan. Prataprao decided to go alone and capture Bahlol Khan but 6 of his soldiers decided to join him. He sat on his horse and they started to go towards Bahlol Khan. Bahlol Khan was crossing a pass in Naseri. Prataprao saw them and penetrated inside Bahlol Khan's army. Bahlol Khan's army saw the Marathas and came to fight them. Prataprao and the 6 soldiers gave a really good fight. Prataprao saw his soldiers were losing so he came beside them and started fighting. He took a sword from the enemy and started using that sword also. Prataprao saw that one of his Mavala had got a big wound. He ordered two of his soldiers to take care of him. Prataprao stood ahead of the wounded soldier and started attacking Bahlol Khan's soldiers. All six got wounded and were not able to fight. Prataprao was wounded but he was making sure no one got close to the wounded soldiers. After some time, they were ready to fight again. Seven daredevil Marathas got up and started fighting again. Now they were fighting really great. They tried very hard to come close to Bahlol Khan but the other good warriors from his side stopped them. They put up a huge fight but it was not enough to stop the 20,000 army. Finally all seven of them were killed.

This happened on February 24, 1674. Shivaji felt extremely bad about this. He had huge respect for Prataprao and his bravery. Shivaji built a statue for him.

Shivaji always felt bad about his treatment of Paratprao. He thought, "Prataprao Gujar fought bravely for me, looted villages, made surat give us half the money that they used to give Aurangzeb and what did Prataprao get in return ? Death. I should not have shown such a bad temper with Prataprao Gujar. I shouldn't have done that." But nobody could bring back the brave Prataprao. He sacrificed his life for Swarajya.

Chapter 28

Bahlol Khan runs away.

S hivaji wanted to get rid of Bahlol Khan and Diler Khan. They were troubling the common people. Diler Khan was busy in the Kangera fort. Shivaji started thinking of defeating Bahlol Khan once and for all. Shivaji called Anandrao Makaji and Moropant. They discussed a way of defeating Bahlol. They tried once before but they were badly defeated. This time they decided to win at any cost. Anandrao was very smart and he came up with an idea. He went to Bahlol Khan Jahangir with few soldiers and told them, "We need to defeat Bahlol Khan. ,ATTACK BAHLOL Khan's CITY AND LOOT IT AND WHEN BAHLOL Khan REALIZE THIS HE WILL HAVE TO RUN TO HIS JAHAGIR. WE WILL GO BACK AND KEEP OUR SOLDIERS READY!" His soldiers saluted and they went towards the city. They looted every single house except the poor. Soon they sent a letter to Bahlol Khan. It said, "Oh Bahlol Khan. You are losing your own Jahagir and you are sitting there eating, drinking and troubling Shivaji. We will loot the whole city and get all the people on our side." Bahlol Khan was shocked and took all his soldiers towards his Jahagir. The Maratha soldiers looted the city and ran away back to Maharashtra. Bahlol Khan was very furious. He said, "Why do these Marathas do all this? I shall defeat them." Bahlol Khan wanted to go back but then he got the news that the Marathas were ready for him. He found out that he could be defeated and he got scared. He decided that he shall defeat the Marathas one day but before he could do that, he got sick and then he forgot what he said and before he could remember it, he died.

Chapter 29

Diler Khan runs away.

Diler Khan was surrounding the fort Kangera when he got an attack from the Maratha soldiers. The Marathas had 700 soldiers and Diler Khan had 10,000 soldiers. Diler Khan tried his best to defeat the Maratha soldiers. The Marathas surrounded him. Then some more Marathas came. A big battle started between the two armies.

Ramoji Pangera was the main soldier fighting from the Maratha side. He was fighting fiercely. Ramoji started searching everywhere for Diler Khan. Ramoji Pangera finally saw Diler Khan. Diler Khan was scared. He was hiding in his tent. He saw his soldiers were falling. He was shocked and finally went up to fight. When Ramoji pangera saw this,

Ramoji Pangera and some of his friends started chasing Diler Khan. A Mughal soldier noticed this and started aiming arrows at Ramoji. Unfortunately, one arrow hit Ramoji Pangera. Ramoji fell off his horse and died.

The Marathas still were not scared. They showed ten times the bravery they were fighting before. Soon Diler Khan's army started losing the battle and he was wounded too. He ran for his life. Then he wrote a letter to Aurangzeb. It said to Auranzeb, "These Marathas are not ordinary soldiers, these are ghosts. You could never understand how they suddenly appear from nowhere. They were able to defeat me in a fair battle. They killed 3,000 of our soldiers."

When Shivaji got the news he was happy. His brave Maratha soldiers were able to defeat a big army but he was sad because Ramoji, his childhood friend, had to lose his life. Ramoji Pangera was not just just a friend of Shivaji but also was a high ranked officer in Shivaji's army who helped Shivaji tackle Afzal Khan.

Chapter 30

Shivaji wins Pandavgad.

It had been a week since Ramoji Pangera's death. One day, Shivaji thought of winning Pandavgad. He had won that fort in the same year when he won Torna.

That fort had been captured by the Bijapurkar soldiers. Bijapurkar soldiers surrounded the fort for one whole year. The Marathas had to surrender the fort.

Shivaji always wanted to win the fort back from the Bijapurkar. One day, he sent Hansaji Mohite and Vithoji Shinde. Hansaji and Vithoji took a few Maratha soldiers with them and went to win Pandavgad Fort. Hansaji took a bow and arrow. Vithoji took a rope and two swords. They reached the bottom of Pandavgad. Hansaji took an arrow and tied a rope to it. He shot the arrow to the top. They pulled it two times to check if it was stuck properly. Hansaji took the rope and climbed up. When the Marathas reached the top the Bijapurkars soldiers shouted, "The Marathas have come." One of the Bajpurkar soldiers saw Hansaji climbing, he was about to aim an arrow at the rope but Hansaji was very quick, he saw the soldier and threw an arrow at him. The enemy fell and the Marathas started attacking. Hansaji was battling many soldiers. There was a cliff. Shinde was fighting over there. Shinde was also wounded. Many people attacked him that he had to back up and his legs came on the edge. Then he attacked everyone at once and the Bajpurkar soldiers were shocked. Shinde was swinging his swords furiously. He saw that he was losing many Marathas every minute. He knew that if this goes on, they will lose many more Marathas. Shinde saw this and started swinging his swords everywhere so he can kill as many Bijapurkars as we can. Hansaji took his bow and arrow and went to fight with the fort keeper. He aimed an arrow at the fort keeper. The fort keeper was running towards Shinde. Hansaji was unable to aim because the fort keeper kept running. Hansaji took his bow and arrow and prayed to Lord Shiva. He shot the arrow and it hit the fort keeper. The fort keeper fell. Then, Vithoji Shinde also fell but after killing almost all the Bijapurkars. The battle ended.

Shivaji came to the fort when he heard the news. He asked, "Where is Vithoji Shinde?" Hansaji said, "Vithoji died while fighting. Many Bijapurkar soldiers surrounded him. He managed to kill all of them but then he was hit by an arrow and he died. I was able to kill the fort keeper and win the fort but I was not able to save Vithoji." Shivaji felt bad but then he said, "Hansaji. I found the correct chief military commander. It is about time that I honor you for your bravery. I will change your name from Hansaji and to Hambirrao which means your Majesty. You are worth this honor." Hambirrao could not say anything. He was speechless with this respect and love from Shivaji. He just bowed humbly. Shivaji gave him new clothes and a new turban with a jewel inside.

Swarajya got its new chief military commander who was dedicated and brave to protect it from enemy.

Chapter 31

Shivaji is crowned.

Shivaji was really sad when Prataprao died but then the news came that everything was planned for his crowning ceremony. Then he got a letter from Ramoji Dattao. It said, "Maharaj, the throne is ready. It is about time that you should have a crowning ceremony. "

Shivaji visited Jijamata. She was in Pachad at that time. He requested Jijamata to come with him to see the throne. Both Shivaji and Jijamata went to Raigad Fort. When he saw the throne, he was astonished. The throne had many jewels and was made of gold. Shivaji appreciated the efforts of Ramoji. He rewarded Ramoji with 10, 000 Rupees. But then Shivaji asked, "Why did you put so many jewels on this throne? It reminds me of my dear friend Prataprao who I lost recently. " He kept on thinking if it was worth to spend almost 40,000 Hon on this throne.

But everyone was excited for the Crowning ceremony. Everyone around him wanted to see him become a king.

One month before the ceremony, he got the news that a pundit named Gaga Bhatt was coming to visit Shivaji. When Gaga Bhatt reached Rajasthan, Shivaji sent 1,000 people with an elephant. When Gaga Bhatt reached Raigad Fort, Shivaji got ready to meet Gaga Bhatt. A soldier asked, "Should I arrange for a horse?" Shivaji said, "No. I will walk." When Shivaji saw Gaga Bhatt, he immediately fell at Gaga Bhatt's feet. Gaga Bhatt was happy to see Shivaji's humble nature. Shivaji walked up to Raigad and brought a horse which was never used. He put a nice cloth on it and put some soldiers next to it. Then he led it to Gaga Bhatt. Gaga Bhatt thanked Shivaji for all the respect Shivaji had shown to him. Gaga Bhatt rode up to the fort. Gaga Bhatt stayed there for two months.

After a month Gaga Bhatt woke up to the Mawle blowing horns and banging drums. He knew that auspicious day was here. It was the first day of Shivaji's crowning ceremony. He woke up and went to the royal treasury and told the guards his plan. They agreed. They let him in. He did a Namaskar to the gold and then took out big earthen pots from the closet nearby. He filled the pots with gold and took them to the court. Shivaji was seated on a couch. The Mawle started blowing horns. Gaga Bhatt was offered royal clothes and then he walked up to Shivaji. He lifted a handful of gold from the pots and sprinkled it on Shivaji. Then after it was done, people came for entertainment. Then Shivaji asked, "Where is Shambhu Raje and Rajaram.?" Sambhaji and Rajaram were watching from a gallery. They came running in. Gaga Bhatt sprinkled some gold on them too.

Next couple of days were filled with entertainment programs. On the fourth day Shivaji woke up at 4 in the morning. Shivaji had brought the throne to Raigad and today he was going to sit on it. He woke up.

He wore his best clothes and put on his turban which had a jewel in it. Exactly at 4:45 everyone gathered up. Shivaji walked up to the throne. He bowed to it and then he looked. At five in the morning, he sat on the throne. At the same time, the Marathas blew cannons from every fort. 10,000 thousand people attended the coronation.

A British soldier named Henry Oxenden came to Raigad. He asked Shivaji three questions. First, can we put our camps in Maharashtra, Mumbai? Shivaji said yes. The second question was that could they put their soldiers to guard their camp? Shivaji also said yes. The last question was that would the british currency work in Maharashtra? Shivaji said no to that. He said, "This is not any kingdom where anyone can use any type of currency. In my kingdom, only Hones will be used."

Shivaji sat on an elephant and Hambirrao Mohite was Mahaut for a day. People showered flowers on Shivaji as he went. Shivaji went all the way till Pachad and then he stopped his elephant. He walked up to Jijamata. She said, "You fulfilled my wish. I was able to see our own Swarajya because of you.All my dreams have come true. I am ready to die now." Shivaji said, "Do not say anything like this Maa Saheb." Both of them just sat there holding each other's hand for a while. This moment was speaking a thousand words without any conversation. Both of them saw a dream which seemed impossible at the time but it finally became the reality. After some time, Shivaji did a namaskar to Jijamata and went back to Raigad.

When the guests went back to their homes, they saw that Raigad fort's entrance was so big that you could put a hut on top of an elephant and a Maratha flag on top. When Henry went back to the British camps, he wrote about the coronation of Shivaji and they spent so much money that they might attack Surat once more. It says, "Shivaji was really kind to me. If I was in Aurangzeb or in any other king's court and I would have asked those questions, the king would have taken me out of his court but Shivaji stayed calm and just told me to not ask these questions again and if I did, I would be given a punishment. Shivaji's court was almost filled with gold. They had spent 40 hundred thousand hons in the coronation. I thought that the court is built of gold. I think that the other fort also has this much gold. If we are going to colonize India, we will get so much money because if one state has so much money, we will get a lot of money: 20 palaces, 20,000 houses, and 300 statues can approximately be made by the gold of Maharashtra."

After the crowning ceremony, he was not just Shivaji, he became Chatrapati Shivaji Maharaj, a true magnificent king of Maharashtra.

Chapter 32

Demise of Jijamata.

It had been eleven days since Shivaji was crowned. One day, Shivaji was talking with his Sardars. Just then, A messenger came. He did a mujra to Shivaji. "Come in," Shivaji said. Shivaji looked at the messenger's face. The messenger had a worried look. Tears rolled down his eyes. The messenger said, "Maharaj. Jijamata is very sick. Quickly come and visit her. Shivaji took his horse and rode towards Pachad. When Shivaji reached, he got off his horse. He ran in where Jijamata was. She said, "My son. It is time, I need to go away. My dreams have come true." Shivaji had tears in his eyes. He sent a messenger to get Sambhaji. Soyarabai and Rajaram were already there. Sambhaji came in. Jijabai said, "Shambhu, how great

73

is it to see you. Take care of yourself." Sambhaji came close and sat next to Jijabai. After some time, many other soldiers came and stood around Jijabai. Then Jijabai uttered her last words, "May you succeed in defeating the Mughals, Adil Shahi, and Nizam Shah. Sambhaji, may you become a nice and perfect king. Rajaram, may you be a wise and smart king like Shivaji. All the Rani Saheb's, take care of Shivaji and your children." Saying this, Jijabai took her last breath. Shivaji fell at Jijabai's feet. Sambhaji shouted, "Grandmother". Tears rolled from everyone's eyes. Soon, people brought a funeral pyre. They lit fire in it. People gathered around. When the mawale put Jijabai in the fire, Shivaji bowed to Jijamata. Shivaji felt very sad. People offered flowers in the funeral pyre. Jijamata passed away on 17 June 1674.

Shivaji had lost a great support. Jijamata inspired Shivaji to build Swarajya. Shivaji knew that if Jijamata was still alive, she would have inspired Shivaji to expand his kingdom, but, alas,nobody could bring back Jijamata.

Chapter 33

Mohammad Quli Khan returns to Shivaji.

Do you know the real name of Mohhamad Khan? He was actually Netoji Palkar. After Shivaji Maharaj escaped from Agra, Aurangzeb captured Netoji Palkar. He was fighting alongside Mirza Raje at that time. Aurangzeb made Netoji fight for him. He even changed Netoji's name to Mohhamad Khan. Netoji had been fighting in Kabul for 9 years. Aurangzeb made sure he did not run away.

After the attack on Kabul Aurangzeb asked his army, "Who will beat Shivaji? Shahistya Khan failed, Bahadur Khan failed, Diler

Khan failed, Daud Khan and Ikhalas Khan failed, Inayat Khan just got scared, Syed Abdullah could not defeat him. Only Mirza Raje managed to defeat Shivaji but now, he was also no more. Who has the courage to defeat Shivaji?" Just then, Aurangzeb thought of a brave warrior. He was called Prati Shivaji (Shivaji's replica) at one point. He was no other than Mohhamad Quli Khan. He was 6 feet tall and had strong muscles.

Aurangzeb said, "Mohhamad Quli Khan! Go and attack Shivaji. Do not think of escaping and joining Shivaji again. I am watching you. I will send Diler Khan with you." Mohhemad Quli Khan did a Mujra and left.

Mohammed Quli Khan took his 300 Marathas and 300 Pathans. Diler Khan and Netoji left for Maharashtra. During their travel, Diler Khan troubled him a lot. He put him in a cage and let him free only when they were going through Shivaji's kingdom. Finally they reached the area. Shivaji maharaj got the news.

Netoji was continuously thinking about the ways to escape and get back to Shivaji Maharaj. One day, Netoji Palkar got his 300 Mawle and said, "These Mughals are bad. Why should we work for them? Let's attack them and run away." One night Netoji Palkar and his 300 Marathas escaped. Some Pathans saw them. They started shouting, "The kafirs are running away. Catch them!" Diler Khan sent 500 soldiers on horses. The Marathas hid in an area. It was dark so the Mughals were having a tough time to see. Netoji was used to it because he fought Mughals hundreds of times like this in the night. When the Mughals reached, Netoji took some arrows and aimed them towards the horses legs. One maratha lit an arrow on fire and Netoji let the arrow go. The arrow hit the horse's leg and the horse started panicking. The Mughals were also scared. Netoji attacked and wiped out the Mughals. Netoji took two swords in his hand and started swinging them. Netoji's

Mawle distracted the Mughals allowing Netoji to run. The Mughals were swinging their swords furiously. 100 Marathas died and 50 were wounded. When they told Diler Khan, he was so mad. When Netoji wanted to get in touch with Shivaji maharaj, the Marathas thought he was a Mughal. He hid in the bushes. The left 200 Marathas came back and Netoji went in there. When Maharaj came, he fell at his feet. He said "I am Netoji Palkar. I was captured by Aurangzeb. I want to take my job back and serve you with all my power. Shivaji Raje said, "I value your loyalty. I can not give your job back . The new commander is Hambirrao Mohitte but I can give you a better job. You can be one of my main bodyguards. I trust you with my life." Netoji did a Mujra. Shivaji said "Come on, Let's hold a naming ceremony to name you back to Netoji". Netoji joined Shivaji once again. He came home and Raje welcomed him with open arms.

Chapter 34

First loot of
Bahadur Khan Kokaltash.

S hivaji maharaj got the news that Bahadur Khan, who was
defeated in the battle of Salher had returned. Before Shivaji
was born, Bahadur Khan brought victory to Shah Jahan in every war.
As a honor, Shah Jahan changed his name from Kokaltash Khan to
Bahadur Khan. He tried defeating Shivaji but he lost. Bahadur Khan
was camping in Burhanpur. Bahadur Khan was attacked by Shivaji and
was defeated. Soon, he got a letter from Aurangzeb. It said, "Bahadur
Kokaltash! Take Siva and bring him to me or I will kill you." Bahadur
Khan felt bad but also mad. He sent a letter to Aurangzeb, "Oh you
foolish king. You were not able to keep Shivaji in Agra, You tried it

yourself, you were not able to capture Shivaji for long. You have all these guards, horsemen, cannons and elephants and still you were not able to stop Shivaji from expanding his kingdom. Shivaji flew like a bird on your watch. What should I do about that?" Aurangzeb was furious.

Here in Maharashtra, Shivaji Maharaj got the news that Bahadur Khan had a lot of money. He told Hambirrao Mohitte to capture Bahadur Khan and get all his money. Hambirrao went with 9,000 soldiers. He told 2,000 of his soldiers to attack first. The whole army went after them. The 2,000 Marathas started running in one direction. The Mughals started chasing them. Hambirrao along with his soldiers attacked the remaining Mughal soldiers and fought with them. Hambirrao sat on his horse and went on a hill. He took his bow and arrow and called another soldier. He took some fire and put it on Hambirrao's arrow. Hambirrao let the arrow go and then he shot more arrows which were lit on fire on the Mughal tents. The Mughals chasing the 2,000 Marathas soon saw smoke rising near their camp. The Mughals rode back to the tent. Some Marathas saw dust rising up from the side the Mughals were so they alerted the Marathas. The Marathas killed all the Mughals who were left and looted as much as they could but they did not have much time so they were only able to loot 20,000 hons. Mughals still had 300,000 hons left in their tents. When the Mughals chasing the Marathas reached their tents, they were shocked to see that their whole camp was burnt and the people who were left at the camp dead. The Mughals searched for a clue but the Marathas were so swift that the Mughals did not find a single clue. The Marathas were now planning their next move and were talking about something extraordinary which was to loot Bahadur Khan one more time.

Chapter 35

Padmadurg

Shivaji raje had thought of winning Janjira many times. But he was not successful. One day he decided to build a fort near Janjira. The fort was built on an island called Kasa. The construction of the fort started in 1676. It was ten miles away from Janjira.

Shivaji ordered Daulat Khan and Kanhoji Angre to surround the fort and protect it from Siddi. Atleast 5,000 people were there at the fort. It included people building the fort and the navy to protect it. After some days, they started running out of money to build the fort. Shivaji sent a letter to Jiwaji Vinayak, a Subedar of a village nearby. The letter said, "Our men need food and money. Please send money to them. I request you to help the people complete the construction."

Jiwaji did not send the money. He simply ignored the request. Then, a strict letter came from Shivaji. It said, "Our men are fighting with Siddi. They are not even caring about their lives. They are trying their best to defend Siddi from stopping the construction. If they do not get money, they will not get food. If they do not get food, they will die. Have you decided to work for the Habshis'(The siddis.) I am giving you a warning, Jiwaji. If you do not send the money, I will not even hesitate to throw you in jail."

Jiwaji got scared. He immediately sent money. Some months later, the construction of the fort finished.

Shivaji maharaj named the fort Padmadurg because it was shaped like a flower. Padmadurg means flower fort in marathi. Now the construction was done and now it was time to win Janjira.

Chapter 36

Second looting of Bahadur Khan.

Bahadur Khan had gone to Delhi and now Aurangzeb sent him back with a huge army and 20,000 hons. Shivaji found this out. He smiled. He readied his soldiers and discussed a plan. Shivaji sent a letter to Bahadur Khan. This is the english translation: "You are very strong. You are very great. We can not fight anymore. We will give you our money and Swarajya and our lives. We shall fall at Alamgir's feet. Reading this, Bahadur Khan was happy. He immediately sent a letter to Aurangzeb:Shivaji had surrendered. We are getting stronger. More steps to go and then you are king of Hindustan. Aurangzeb got happy and sent Bahadur Khan 80,000 hon. The Adil shahi kingdom was defeated by the Mughals. Diler Khan had been made the chief of Deccan but then he made Bahadur Khan chief. Shivaji went and won Karnataka and other parts of Dakshin. That mission is called Dakshin Digvijay which means conquest of the south. Shivaji went back to Maharashtra and kept Hambirrao near Karwar. After some days, Hambirrao got the news that Bahadur Khan was camping in Karwar. He was planning a surprise attack on the marathas. Hambirrao discussed the plan of the Mughals. A maratha said, "How will we be able to face Bahadur Khan? He had 20,000 soldiers?" Hambirrao said, "Whoever enters a lion's territory either dies or runs away. We will be like lions." On the new moon, Hambirrao took 5,000 soldiers and attacked Bahadur Khan on the dead of night. The Mughals shouted ``The Ganim have come!''Before the soldiers could be ready, Hambirrao looted the whole camp as fast as a hurricane and just rode away with the 10,0000 hons leaving the Mughals in a cloud of dust. When Shivaji saw the loot, he patted Hambirrao on the back. He had now got 10,0000 hons, one elephant, 9,000 soldiers and much more.

Chapter 37

Janjira one more time.

For the last 20 years, Shivaji was thinking of how to win Janjira. This was the one fort that eluded him forever.

When Moropant returned from a mission, Shivaji told him to win Janjira. Moropant nodded and said, "I will not return until I win Janjira."

Moropant tried attacking Janjira in many different ways but he couldn't succeed. He made a big tower and put some big cannons on them. He blew many cannonballs to break a hole in Janjira. He was thinking if he could make a hole in Jajira, his Mawle would sneak in. But he could not break a hole with cannons.

He then met with his sardars and decided a plan. He decided that they would put ladders on Janjira. The Marathas would climb on those ladders and enter Janjira. Once the Marathas are in, they would help the rest of the army get inside. But they could not even put the ladders and this plan failed. It was extremely difficult to get inside the fort.

Many people tried but they failed. Moropant was not able to figure out a plan to enter Janjira Fort. Moropant then met a fisherman named Lay Patil. Moropant asked him for help. Lay patil agreed to help him. They decided to try the ladder strategy again but now with the help of brave Lay Patil and his men. Lay Patil thought of how to do it. He took 100 soldiers to guard if anyone attacks. No one knows how he went and how he put the ladders but he must have taken some experts who are good at climbing and they climbed up and put the ladders. Lay patil put the ladders to fort Janjira, and waited for the Marathas to come. The plan was that the Maraths would come and climb those ladders and then get inside the fort. The Marathas could not bring torches or they would be seen. They had to travel only in moonlight. They were sailing towards the fort Janjira in the dark. Unfortunately, they lost their way and went in the wrong way. Lay patil did not know that. He waited for them for 5 hours. Now it was almost dawn. Lay patil had to take down the ladders and sail away. The Marathas finally found the way but Lay patil had gone back with the ladders. Siddi's guard could now see everything in bright daylight. The Marathas had no choice but to retreat.

This was a very unfortunate incident. The Marathas would have won the fort if they could reach the fort on time. Moroapnt was sad so he went back. Shivaji was also sad but he was amazed by Lay patil's bravery. He praised Lay patil for his extraordinary bravery and asked him, "Who made you Patil?" The Patil answered, "The Badshah". Shivaji Raje was amazed and honored him with name Sarpatil. Jajira was still one fort that Shivaji Maharaj could never win.

Chapter 38

Nagoji Jedhe

Complaints were coming from Karnataka about Miyana Hussain Khan. Shivaji Raje decided to conquer Hussain Khan's area. Hambirao Mohite went to win the area with 10,000 army. Nagoji Jedhe was one of them. He came with his father, Surjerao Jedhe (Baji jedhe).He was the grandson of Kanhoji Jedhe and the son of Baji Jedhe. Nagoji was only 17 but he was ready for the fight. Another one was Dhanaji Jadhav. He was very tall and strong. When they were marching through Yelburga, they got an attack from Hussain Khan. Nagoji fought and fought. First, the Marathas were winning. Hambirrao was leading the Mawle. He told Nagoji and Sarjerao to try to kill Hussain Khan. Bijapurkars came up and put up a fight with

Hambirrao. Nagoji saw this. He got mad. He picked up his pistol and aimed it at the Bijapurkars soldier. He shot the bullet and it hit right in the enemies stomach. The Bijapurkars screamed with pain. He tried to get up but he could not. It was almost night. Hussain Khan climbed on his elephant and tried running away. His soldiers circled him for protection and they started moving away. Nagoji and Surjerao saw this. Nagoji said to Baji, "Father. I will go in and make chaos in there. Then you take cannons and aim them at the army. Baji said yes. Nagoji touched his father's feet. Baji put him on a horse and gave him a bow and arrow. He gave him his quiver to keep the arrows in. Nagoji Jedhe mounted on the horse and went. Nagoji went into the army. He made sure none of his arrows fell. He rode into the enemy's camp and put poison on the arrows. He rode out of the camp. Few Bijapurkar soldiers came ahead. Nagoji took his sword out of his scabbard. Nagoji took his sword and cut the enemy's hand. In all that, his sword was hit so hard that it broke. Nagoji took a stick from the ground. He hit the sticks fiercely on Hussain Khan's soldiers. Then Nagoji came near the elephant Hussain Khan was sitting on. He took his bow and arrow and hit the arrow in the elephant's trunk. He took another one and aimed it on the head. Nagoji took his third arrow and was about to aim it towards Hussain Khan when Hussain Khan shot an arrow at Nagoji but it missed. Nagoji also hit the arrow aiming at Hussain Khan. The arrow hit the Mahaut and the Mahaut died. Hussain Khan shot another arrow. Nagoji saw the arrow and put his shield in front of the arrow. Hussain Khan got mad. He aimed 5 arrows and let them go at a great speed. Nagoji took his shield up. It guarded his body but not his head. One of the arrows hit Nagoji on the head and Nagoji fell down. He became unconscious. Then Dhanaji Jadhav took Nagoji's place and surrounded the elephant. The elephant had been hit by so many arrows with poison that it weakend. The Elephant started running away. In all this, Hussain Khan dropped ladders down and started climbing down. He finally reached the bottom. Dhanaji Jadhav wiped out the army around Hussain Khan and captured him. The elephant created havoc in the army of the Bijapurkars. The soldiers, scared of getting under the elephant's legs, ran away. Baji Jedhe finally came up to Nagoji and saw he was almost dead. Nagoji opened his eyes and looked at his father. He was too weak to keep his eyes open. Baji Jedhe tried taking the arrow out of his head but it was too late. Nagoji died in his father's arms. Nagoji was only 17 when he died. He was young but brave. He sacrificed his life for Swarajya. He inspired thousand other Marathas to continue the fight for Swarajya.

Chapter 39

Meeting Qutub Shah and Yesaji's fight with the elephant.

Shivaji Maharaj had new plans to win the Badshah's area. There were new events happening in Bijapur. Bahlol Karim Khan was Wazir. Bahlol Khan killed Prataprao Gujar a few years back. He had also killed Khavas Khan. Khavas Khan was looking after Adil Shah's kingdom because Adil Shah's son was just a child. Recently, Bahlol Khan died and Siddi Masud became the Wazir. Siddi Masud was responsible for the fight in Ghodkhind. He killed Baji Prabhu Deshpande.

Shivaji Maharaj had a great vision for Swarajya. He thought if all the kingdoms in South India can unite together, they can form a great army and fight with the Badshah as a united front. He decided to talk to Qutub Shah and convince him to conquer the Karnataka area together. Shivaji decided to go to Hyderabad. Qutub Shah got scared. He knew what happened to Afzal Khan. He did not want to die with the same feet. Shivaji sent a letter to Qutub Shah. He wrote, "You do not need to be scared. I do not trouble the ones who are not my enemies. I do not want to fight those who do not trouble my people."

Qutub Shah was a little bit relieved. He agreed to meet Shivaji Maharaj. Shivaji Maharaj went to see Qutub Shah. He was treated with respect by Qutub Shah. Shivaji Maharaj was a king himself now and he was treated as the king should be treated. Shivaji Maharaj also showed Qutub Shah the same respect. He made friends with Qutub shah and said, "I need your help. We can join hands and defeat the Bijapurkars kingdom." Qutub Shah asked Shivaji Maharaj, "How many elephants do you have? I have 1,000. Shivaji said, "I have around 30,000 elephants. "Qutub Shah was shocked. Shivaji laughed. He said, "My Mawles are like powerful elephants. My one mawala is as powerful as an elephant." Qutub Shah said, "Can one of your Marathas defeat an Elephant?" Shivaji Maharaj remembered his dear friend Tanaji. Tanaji fought with Udaybhan's elephant and made him surrender himself. But unfortunately, Tanaji was no more. But, then Shivaji Maharaj thought of Yesaji Kank. He was a brave soldier.

He asked Yesaji if he would fight an elephant. Yesaji Kank did not hesitate even for a second. He said, "Your order is my command."

Yesaji Kank prepared himself for a fight and jumped in the arena. Yesaji looked up. Everyone closed their eyes. They thought he fell in by mistake. From the other door came a killer elephant. Shivaji looked at Yesaji. Yesaji saw the elephant. He took out his Dandpatta and spun it around. He climbed all the way up the huge wall and tied a rope to the top. Then he jumped down again. The elephant came charging towards Yesaji. Yesaji dodged the elephant and the elephant bumped into the wall. Yesaji went far and held his rope. The elephant took its head out of the wall and came back to Yesaji. Yesaji jumped on the wall. The elephant came back towards Yesaji. Yesaji jumped on the elephant. He took his spears and put it in the elephants back. Yesaji swinged back on the wall. He came back and cut the elephant's trunk. The elephant started panicking. Yesaji came back and put his spears in the elephant's chest. The elephant fell down and died. Yesaji came out and shouted, "See. I did it."

Warning : Do not do this to animals. This is very violent.

Shivaji Maharaj walked up to Yesaji. Yesaji did a Mujra. Shivaji hugged Yesaji and said, "Nice job Yesaji. You are a brave soldier." Even Qutub Shah was impressed and he told Shivaji Maharaj that he is lucky to have so many brave soldiers. Shivaji Maharaj said, "It is time to attack Bijapur." Shivaji Maharaj took his 10,000 soldiers and Qutub Shah took his 10,000 soldiers. They decided to win the entire Karnataka. It was a grand plan.

Chapter 40

Jinji

Shivaji maharaj wanted to win the Fort Jinji. Jinji was one of the strongest forts. It was so strong that in case of a siege, it could stand undefeated for as long as 6 years. The fort Jinji was in the Adil Shahi kingdom.

Shivaji took 20,000 of his army. 10,000 people on horse and 10,000 people on foot. Shivaji brought cannons along with him. Shivaji surrounded Jinji. The fort keeper was Nasir Mauhhamed Khan. One day, the Marathas went to meet Khan. Khan greeted them and asked, "What are you here for?" The Marathas said, "If you surrender the fort and accept a Jahagir, you will get 50,000 hon. But if you deny our request, you will have to accept perish and wrath. Nasir Mauhhamed surrendered the fort. Jinji was now part of Swarajya.

Now Shivaji turned his attention to Vellore fort. That fort was a very important fort. Vellore had water around it. The fort keeper, Abdul Khan had put crocodiles in the water. Shivaji surrounded Vellore. Shivaji tried winning this fort but he was not successful. He built two forts near Vellore named Sajra and Gojra. Shivaji put cannons on top of those forts and tried to aim them at Vellore fort but it still would not work. Nasir Muhammad told Abdul Khan to give the fort but Abdur Khan did not surrender. Shivaji thought of winning Vellore another time. He decided to focus on it another time.

Shivaji then got the news that Sher Khan had a huge Jahagir. Sher Khan himself was not a great warrior but was very smart. Shivaji left Vellore and came near Sher Khan's Jahagir. Sher Khan got the news that Shivaji had come. He made his soldiers ready because he knew that using guerilla warfare, Shivaji can attack anytime. The Marathas thought that Sher Khan was going to attack so they were also ready. Some weeks passed. Shivaji still did not attack. Sher Khan thought that he should attack now. He and his son Ibrahim Khan took their army and went where Shivaji was camping. Sher Khan saw that he would not be able to defeat Shivaji if he attacked so he started retreating. He thought that Shivaji would not chase them. Shivaji saw Sher Khan was retreating. The Marathas got on their horses and started fighting with Sher Khan. 900 people from Sher Khan's army ran away. 500 fought but were instantly defeated. Sher Khan and Ibrahim Khan ran away. The Marathas caught them. They took him to Shivaji. Shivaji welcomed him. Sher Khan said, "I will give you a Jahagirs if you accept."

Conquering Jinji and defeating Sher Khan was a big win for Shivaji Maharaj and Swarajya.

Chapter 41

Vyankoji Raje defeats Santaji.

Shivaji maharaj had won everything except Bangalore. He sent a letter to Vyankoji Raje. Shivaji Maharaj was hoping that Vyankoji Raje would help him in his fight for Swarajya. But Vyankoji Raje never really supported him. Shivaji Maharaj tried to convince him one more time. He sent a letter to Vyankoji Raje. It said, "Please give us money, horses, elephants, and soldiers.If you help us we will be grateful." Vyankoji Raje was jealous of Shivaji Maharaj. He refused to help Shivaji Maharaj. He thought of using guerrilla warfare against the Marathas. He readied his 1,000 Bijpurkars and started marching onto Shivaji Raje's army.

Hambirrao found this out and decided to fight him. He told Santaji to ride towards Vyankoji Raje and attack him. Santaji went with his

1,000 soldiers. He hid in the bush. When Vyankoji arrived, the Marathas hurled stones at them from every side. The Bijapurkars were confused. They stood in a strong battle formation. Soon, the shouts of Jay Bhawani, Jay Shivaji were heard. The Marathas came out of the bushes and started a battle. Vyankoji was confused. He wondered, "Where did these Marathas come from?" The Bijpurkars attacked. Santaji was holding a bow and arrow and trying to aim the arrows as close to Vyankoji. Santaji saw that his men were dying fast. He sat on his horse and penetrated in the enemy formation. Vyankoji Raje saw him coming towards his soldiers and was shocked to see him, "This Maratha is really brave." Santaji was now killing many Bijpurkars. Vyankoji saw this. He knew that if this went for long, we all would die. He charged his elephant towards the Maratha army and started stomping on the Marathas with his elephant. Santaji sent a messenger to Hambirrao and asked for help. When the messenger reached he told Hambirrao about the situation. Hambirrao took his 4,000 soldiers and went to help. Vyankoji had brought 20,000 Bijapurkar so they were no match. Without thinking what will happen and what will not, Hambirrao rode to the battle. He took his artillery also. When he reached, he blew his cannons. The Bijapurkar were pushed back. But they still kept on fighting. The Bijapurkars were large in numbers. Then the Marathas took their swords and started fighting again. Now Hambirrao tried blowing more cannons but it was no use. The Bijapurkars army had come inside the Maratha formation and if the Marathas blew cannonballs over there, Marathas would die too. Hambirrao thought of a new plan. He rode back to the camps and then told his writer to write a letter to Vyankoji. It said, "Your Majesty. We are really sorry. Please spare us. We will not attack your kingdom again but just spare us today. Our king is really sorry also. We will give you our half of Deccan." Vyankoji Raje read this but he was well aware of this tactic. He knew that there is no truth in this letter. He killed more Marathas but this caused a lot of his soldiers to die too.

Then Hambirrao and Santaji ran away with their left Mawles. A lot of Vyankoji Raje's soldiers had also died so he had to turn around but he captured a small piece of Swarajya. This was a loss to Swarajya.

Then Santaji told Raje about this. He was really ashamed but Shivaji said, "You did the right thing in saving our Mawles. Mawles are our real strength. If we protect them, we can win this lost part again." Santaji felt better but he only had one thing on his mind, winning the lost piece of Swarajya.

Chapter 42

Capturing of Vyankoji Raje.

After Vyankoji Raje attacked Deccan and won it, Santaji Raje and Hambirrao came together and went to attack but they had to retreat. Santaji wanted to take revenge. He sent a letter to Shivaji Raje. It said, "Your brother is riding on the Deccan. He killed 1,000 soldiers. What should I do?" Santaji Raje and Hambirrao waited. After 10 days, he got his answer. Shivaji had written, " He killed 500 Mawle. You want revenge. Don't kill him, instead capture him. They are Marathas."

Santaji Raje and Hambirrao got the news Vyankoji Raje is coming back. He sent a lawyer and a letter. The lawyer gave the letter to Vyankoji Raje. Vyankoji Raje read it out loud. It said, "If you come to Thanjavur, remember, we can attack at any time." Just then, Santaji

Raje and Hambirrao attacked. They had a big battle. Vyankoji Raje was furious. He was reading it when they attacked. He remembered the trick they used before but this one was new. They used the Chakravyuha formation. Both sides were fighting. Vyankoji Raje and his brothers finally surrendered. Santaji Raje and Hambirrao brought him to Shivaji. Vyankoji Raje did not like Shivaji being a king. He thought he was the only king in the family. Rest of the brothers surrendered and joined Shivaji Maharaj. Vyankoji Raje did not like this and told Raje, "Congratulations you are king. I want to go back to Thanjavur." Shivaji Raje felt bad, after all he was his brother. He sent a letter to Vyankoji Raje, " We are all Marathi. I know you have become the king of Thanjavur. Can you give us horses, money and other war material? When I conquer Hindustan a big part of the kingdom will be given to you." Vyankoji Raje was happy and decided to give Shivaji his elephants and cannons. He knew that if Shivaji wins all this, he may become the king of ¼ of his kingdom

Chapter 43

Sambhaji joins Diler Khan.

After the death of Jijamatha, Sambhaji felt alone. She always took care of him as his mother, Saibai passed away when he was just 2. After Jijamatha passed away, Soyarabai started plotting against Sambhaji. She did not want him to become a king after Shivaji Maharaj. Sambhaji was really frustrated due to these tactics. It was too much to bear. He started thinking of joining hands with Mughals. He was also thinking of a plan to expand the kingdom by using the Mughals. He always said that there is no permanent foe or a friend. Nobody could really tell what was going on in his mind. He loved his father and was absolutely dedicated to Swarajya but still decided to join Diler Khan, nobody knew why.

It was night when 5,000 soldiers came to get Sambhaji. Sambhaji was waiting for them. They were Mughals. The Marathas tried putting up a fight but they had only 500 soldiers.

One day Shivaji got a note that Sambhaji was going to come to win the Sahyadris. One day Sambhaji and Diler Khan were marching towards Sayadhris. Meanwhile a baby girl had been born to Yesubai. (Sambhaji's wife). Shivaji decided to name the baby girl Bhavanibai. Meanwhile, Sambhaji was marching towards Bhupalgad. When Sambhaji reached Bhupalgad, Firangoji surrendered because he knew that he would not be able to blow cannons on them. Diler Khan was so cruel that he cut 700 people's hands. When Shivaji got the news he scolded Firangoji. He asked Firangoji why he did not use the cannons. Firangoji told that Sambhaji was leading them. Shivaji was angry yet helpless. He told Firangoji that, "Swarajya always comes first. You shall have a severe punishment." He ordered his soldiers to throw Firangoji off Takmak tok next morning!

When Shivaji was sleeping, he had nightmares. He thought that he should not have said that. Then in the morning, he rushed up to Takmak tok. The guards were not here yet. Then after 1 hour, the guards arrived and Shivaji walked away sadly. But when they were going to drop Firangoji off the cliff, Shivaji ran with his knife and cut off the rope tied on Firangoji's legs and hands. Then Shivaji ordered the soldiers to let Firangoji go. The soldiers let Firangoji go.

Then Shivaji got the news that Diler Khan was attacking villages and looting them. Shivaji did not like this at all. One day Sambhaji disguised himself as a Mawala and rode away from his camp to Panahla. After he reached Panhala, Shivaji met Sambhaji and then Shivaji had to return to Raigad for Rajaram's wedding with the daughter of Prataprao, Jankibai.

Sambhaji was brave but often misunderstood.

Chapter 44

Death of Shivaji Maharaj.

Sambhaji escaped from Diler Khan, and Shivaji and Sambhaji met in 1678. Shivaji had to leave for Raigad fort because of Rajaram's wedding with Jankibai on March 2,1680. The wedding ceremonies went for 5 days. After the ceremony, Shivaji fell ill. Soyarabai did not want Sambhaj to know that the Chatrapatti is ill so she kept Sambhaji on Panhala. Shivaji Maharaj's health was deteriorating by each passing day.

On April 3, 1680, Shivaji sadly passed away. The spies of Sambhaji got the news, and then Sambhaji immediately left for Raigad.

In Raigad, Putalabai was childless and overwhelmed with the death of Shivaji. She immolated herself in Shivaji Maharaj's funeral pyre.

Shivaji's dog Waghya was also very sad about Shivaji's death and jumped in the pyre. Sakwarbai wanted to do the same but she was not allowed to do that because she had a young daughter.

Soyarabai had plans to poison Sambhaji but Sambhaji found out about her intentions and captured Soyarabai. Following this, he put Rajaram under house arrest.

Shivaji was dead but still, the Marathas kept the fight on and expanded Swarajya.

This was the end of Shivaji Maharaj's life but his memory is still preserved. Sambhaji ruled after Shivaji. Later on, Aurangzeb captured and cut off Sambhaji Maharaj's head so after that, Rajaram ruled. When Rajaram died, Tarabai ruled and then Shahu who was Sambhaji's son was let go back to Maharashtra, Swarajya got separated in two pieces. One was ruled by Tarabai because her son was too young. The other piece was ruled by Shahu. When Tarabai died, his son Shivaji II became the ruler of Kolhapur. When Shahu died, his son Rajaram II became king and then the british won Swarajya in November 1817 – February 1818.

Shivaji Maharaj was dead but his memory was kept alive. When Sambhaji got the throne, he built a Samadhi.

Shivbharat came to an end. Shivaji Maharaj was a great king, a true visionary. He was a pioneer king. He was the first one to even think about Swarajya (freedom). These days, we take our freedom granted because we can go anywhere, do anything, talk about anything freely but that was not the case in Mughal's era. Shivaji Maharaj showed his people a dream, that they could be free, they could live freely. It was a huge dream, the one that needed sacrifice. People stood behind him and his vision. They helped him with his life and in return he created Swarajya for his people. His journey to freedom was truly inspirational. He not only ruled the lands of India but also the hearts of the people. He was truly loved and respected by everyone around him. He not only inspired the Marathas while he was alive and ruling but the generation to come.

After more than 400 years, he is still inspiring a small boy like me to read about him, understand him. I consider myself fortunate to know him and call him "The Eternal King".

Printed in Great Britain
by Amazon